INSTANT
Spanish
Vocabulary Builder

TOM MEANS

HIPPOCRENE BOOKS, INC.
NEW YORK

ISBN: 0-7818-0981-9

Book and jacket design by Acme Klong Design, Inc.

For information, address:
Hippocrene Books, Inc.
171 Madison Avenue
New York, NY 10016

Cataloging-in-Publication data available from the Library of Congress.

CONTENTS

Acknowledgments vii
Introduction ix
    Audio Accompaniment. x
    Note on Exercises x
    Note on Answer Key. x
    "False Friends" xi
    Deviations in Spelling xi
Pronunciation Guide xii
Important Note on Gender xiii
Works Consulted. xiv
A Note from the Author xv
A Note to the User xv

	English suffix	Spanish suffix	Page
Chapter 1	–al*	al	1
Chapter 2	–ance	–ancia	15
Chapter 3	–ant	–ante	19
Chapter 4	–ar	–ar	25
Chapter 5	–ary	–ario	29
Chapter 6	–ble	–ble	35
Chapter 7	–ct	–cto	47
Chapter 8	–ence	–encia	53
Chapter 9	–ent**	–ente	61
Chapter 10	–gy	–gía	69
Chapter 11	–ic	–ico	75
Chapter 12	–ical	–ico	89
Chapter 13	–id	–ido	97
Chapter 14	–ism	–ismo	101
Chapter 15	–ist	–ista	109

Chapter 16	–ive	–ivo	117
Chapter 17	–ment	–mento	125
Chapter 18	–or	–or	131
Chapter 19	–ory	–orio	141
Chapter 20	–ous	–oso	145
Chapter 21	–sion	–sión	151
Chapter 22	–sis	–sis	159
Chapter 23	–tion	–ción	165
Chapter 24	–ty	–dad	185

Answer Key... 197

Appendix: CD Track Listing 209

About the Author... 211

*excluding words ending in "–ical," which is a separate Chapter
**excluding words ending in "–ment," which is a separate Chapter

ACKNOWLEDGMENTS

I would like to give special thanks to Juan Pablo Lombana, whose research and bilingual expertise helped make this book possible.

Many thanks to Angelica Bender for her technical assistance with the entire series. Thanks to Ernest Valdés, Enid Bender, Diana Murgio, Dr. Karen Sanchez, John Carleo, and all of my students at Kenneth Cole Productions. Thanks to my editor, Anne Kemper, for her steady and enthusiastic guidance, and also to my former editor, Caroline Gates.

Finally, thanks to all the foreign language teachers who have clearly demonstrated many of these patterns in the past, especially Margarita Madrigal and Michel Thomas.

INTRODUCTION

Instant **Spanish Vocabulary Builder** can add thousands of words to your Spanish vocabulary. It is designed to be a supplement for students of Spanish at all levels. This book will help a student to learn to communicate effectively by dramatically increasing his/her Spanish vocabulary.

There are thousands of English words that are connected to their Spanish counterparts by word-ending patterns. This guide will illustrate those patterns and demonstrate how easily they work. The simple reason is that most of Spanish and much of English is derived from Latin. This means that the two languages share a large number of root words, which makes vocabulary building much easier.

Vocabulary building is one of the keys for successful language learning. This book presents vocabulary patterns between English and Spanish in such a systematic fashion that expanding your vocabulary will be easy and enjoyable. I believe it is the only one of its kind.

Instant Spanish Vocabulary Builder is very easy to use. The 24 patterns presented in this book are based on word-endings (suffixes) and the chapters are listed alphabetically. For example, the first chapter presents English words that end in "–al" (capital, normal, etc.) Many of these words end in "–al" in Spanish also (*capital, normal*, etc.)

The second chapter presents English words that end in "–ance" (distance, importance, etc.) Many of these words correspond to "–ancia" in Spanish (*distancia, importancia*, etc.) In most cases, you only need to slightly change the ending of the English word to arrive at the correct Spanish word. These words are commonly referred to as cognates: words related by common derivation or descent.

AUDIO ACCOMPANIMENT: This book comes with an enclosed compact disc. Every chapter contains many recorded words that typify how words under that pattern are pronounced—all words **in bold** are on the recording. After each Spanish word there will be a pause—it is important for the reader to imitate the native speaker during that pause.

Every chapter also contains common phrases and expressions that are recorded on the audio accompaniment. After every recorded expression there will be a pause for the reader to imitate the native speaker. All expressions **in bold** are on the recording.

In the exercise section of each chapter there are stories for the student to read and listen to with questions that follow. These stories are **in bold** and are also on the recording. They are read by a native speaker at standard speed. Readers are not expected to understand every word of each story, but it is important for language learners to hear new vocabulary words used in an authentic context by a native speaker.

EXERCISES: At the end of every chapter, there are exercises for the reader to do. The first exercise is a matching exercise that reinforces the new words learned in the chapter. The second exercise is a story followed by questions. Every chapter contains a short story about Juan and Angélica, two young Spaniards traveling through Spain.

ANSWER KEY: Answers for the exercises are available in the Answer Key section.

INSTANT Spanish Vocabulary Builder

"FALSE FRIENDS": Sometimes the English word and the Spanish word will look alike and sound alike, but have different meanings. These are often referred to as "false friends" or "false cognates." When this is the case, a more appropriate definition will be provided alongside the translation. One such example can be seen with the English word "parent."

ENGLISH. . . . . SPANISH

parent. . . . . pariente *(meaning "a relative")*

   In some rare cases, the English and Spanish word possess such different meanings that the pair was not included in this book. For example, the meaning of the English word "journal" has no relation to the meaning of the Spanish word *jornal* (day's pay). In other rare cases, overly technical words were not included in this book.

DEVIATIONS IN SPELLING: Precise spelling of the Spanish words may differ from the English words in more ways than just the endings. If you are interested in spelling the word correctly, please pay close attention to the Spanish column. For example,

ENGLISH. . . . . SPANISH

dictionary. . . . . diccionario

PRONUNCIATION GUIDE: *All bolded words in this brief pronunciation guide are recorded on the accompanying CD,* **track 25.**

There are 27 letters in the Spanish alphabet (one more than in the English alphabet). The additional letter is "ñ." Listed below is a brief guide to Spanish pronunciation. English equivalent sounds have been provided whenever possible.

Spanish vowel	Example	Approximate English sound
A	**España**	ah
E	**excelente**	eh
I	**día**	ee
O	**loco**	oh
U	**mucho**	oooh

There are a few pairings that produce distinct sounds that we will go over next:

"ce" and "ci" always produce a soft sound like the English letter "s": **cena** (dinner); **cita** (appointment)

The pairing "ge" produces a soft sound similar to the word "<u>hea</u>d": **gente** (people)
The pairing "gi" produces a sound similar to the word "<u>he</u>": **giro** (turn)

"ca" produces a hard sound similar to the word "<u>car</u>": **casa** (house)
"co" sounds approximately like the beginning of "<u>co</u>lon": **código** (code)
"cu" produces a hard sound similar to the word "<u>coo</u>l": **cubo** (bucket)

"ga" sounds approximately like the beginning of "garbage": **ganar** (to win/to earn)

"go" produces a hard sound similar to the word "going": **gota** (drop)

"gu" produces a hard sound similar to the word "guru": **gula** (gluttony)

"gui" sounds approximately like the word "gear": **guitarra** (guitar)

"gue" produces a hard sound similar to the word "ghetto": **guerrero** (warrior)

The "cc" pairing usually produces a sound similar to "x" in the word "ax": **acción** (action)

The "je" pairing sounds similar to the word "hedge": **jefe** (boss)

The "ll" sounds like the "ll" in "tortilla": **pasillo** (hallway)

The "ñ" sounds like the "ny" in "canyon": **años** (years)

Lastly, the letter "h" is silent in Spanish: **hasta** (until)

IMPORTANT NOTE ON GENDER: Unless otherwise noted in the chapter introduction, all Spanish nouns and adjectives listed in this book are in the singular, masculine form. All nouns are listed without the article that typically accompanies them.

WORKS CONSULTED:

Larousse Diccionario Español-Inglés, Inglés-Español. Primera Edición. México D.F., México: Larousse, 1999.

Merriam-Webster's Collegiate Dictionary, Tenth Edition. Springfield, MA: Merriam-Webster, 2000.

Vox, Diccionario General de la Lengua Española (CD-ROM). Barcelona, Spain: Bibliograf, 1997.

Devney, Dorothy M. *Guide to Spanish Suffixes.* Chicago: Passport Books, 1992.

Knorre, Marty; Dorwick, Thalia; Perez-Girones, Ana Maria; Glass, William R.; Villareal, Hildebrando. *Puntos de Partida, Fifth Edition.* Boston: McGraw-Hill, 1997.

Madrigal, Margarita. *Margarita's Magical Key to Spanish.* New York: Doubleday, 1989.

Prado, Marcial. *NTC's Dictionary of Spanish False Cognates.* Chicago, NTC Publishing Group, 1993.

Thomas, Michel. *Spanish with Michel Thomas.* Chicago: NTC Publishing Group, 2000.

A NOTE FROM THE AUTHOR

When I first started studying Spanish, I translated an old trick I had learned from Italian: most English words that end in "–tion" stay the same in Spanish but their ending changes to "–ción." I was soon confidently speaking of the new "*situación*" that I had seen at the "*estación*," or about the "*condición*" of this or that. I was convinced that I had found the "*solución*" to speaking Spanish!

I know that this vocabulary bridge aided my Spanish skills greatly and fed my enthusiasm for learning and using a beautiful language.

In this book I have collected the 24 most common and applicable vocabulary bridges that exist between English and Spanish. I have done this in the hope that readers find the same immediate application that I did early in my language studies. I hope you find them useful.

A NOTE TO THE USER

The focus of this book is on vocabulary development. However, as with all effective language materials, the vocabulary has been set in an authentic cultural context with realistic characters and stories to encourage immediate applicability in real-life situations.

The exercises are suitable for individual and group work. Teachers will find that the 24 chapters easily can be incorporated into a one-year curriculum.

Chapter 1

Many English words ending in "–al" have the same ending in Spanish (excluding words ending in "–ical," which is a separate pattern).

Spanish words ending in "–al" are usually adjectives or nouns. For example,

artificial (adj.) = *artificial*
animal (n.) = *un animal*

ENGLISH . . . . SPANISH

All words and phrases in bold are on **Track 1** *of the accompanying CD.*

abdominal . . . . abdominal
abnormal . . . . anormal
accidental. . . . . accidental
actual. . . . . actual *(meaning "current, present")*
additional. . . . . adicional
adverbial . . . . adverbial
amoral . . . . amoral
ancestral . . . . ancestral
animal . . . . **animal**
   "It's an animal!" . . . . **"¡Es un animal!"**
annual . . . . anual
antiliberal. . . . . antiliberal
antisocial . . . . antisocial
arsenal. . . . . arsenal
artificial . . . . artificial
asexual . . . . asexual
asocial. . . . . asocial
audiovisual. . . . . audiovisual
autumnal . . . . otoñal

banal	banal
baptismal	bautismal
beneficial	beneficial *(more commonly*
	"beneficioso")
bestial	bestial
biannual	bianual
biennial	bienal
bifocal	bifocal
bilateral	bilateral
bisexual	bisexual
bronchial	bronquial
brutal	**brutal**

"It's a brutal reaction." . . . . . . **"Es una reacción brutal"**.

canal	canal *(also used for "TV channel")*
cannibal	caníbal
capital	**capital** *(for geography, use "la capital";*
	for finance, use "el capital")
cardinal	cardinal
carnal	carnal
carnival	carnaval *(also used for period of*
	Mardi Gras)
casual	casual *(also used for "by chance")*
cathedral	catedral
causal	causal
celestial	celestial
central	**central**
cereal	cereal
cerebral	cerebral
ceremonial	ceremonial
choral	coral
circumstantial	circunstancial
coincidental	coincidencial
collateral	colateral
colloquial	coloquial
colonial	colonial

colossal . . . . colosal
commercial. . . . . comercial
communal. . . . . comunal
conceptual . . . . conceptual
conditional . . . . condicional
confessional . . . . confesional *(only an adjective)*
confidential. . . . . confidencial
confrontational . . . . confrontacional
constitutional. . . . . constitucional
contextual. . . . . contextual
continental . . . . **continental**
contractual . . . . contractual
controversial . . . . controversial
conventional . . . . convencional
conversational. . . . . conversacional
coral . . . . coral
cordial . . . . cordial
corporal . . . . corporal
corral. . . . . corral
correctional . . . . correccional
cranial . . . . craneal
credential . . . . credencial
criminal . . . . criminal
crucial . . . . **crucial**
   "Tomorrow is a crucial day.". . . . . **"Mañana es un día crucial".**
crystal . . . . cristal
cultural. . . . . cultural

decimal . . . . decimal
dental . . . . dental
departmental. . . . . departamental
devotional . . . . devocional
diagonal. . . . . **diagonal**
dictatorial. . . . . dictatorial
differential . . . . diferencial
digital . . . . digital

dimensional . . . . dimensional
disloyal . . . . desleal
divisional . . . . divisional
doctoral . . . . doctoral
dorsal . . . . dorsal
dual. . . . . dual
ducal . . . . ducal
dysfunctional. . . . . disfuncional

editorial . . . . editorial
electoral. . . . . electoral
elemental . . . . elemental *(meaning "elementary")*
emotional . . . . emocional
episcopal . . . . episcopal
equal . . . . **igual**
equatorial. . . . . ecuatorial
essential . . . . esencial
eternal . . . . eternal *(more commonly "eterno")*
eventual . . . . eventual *(meaning "possible")*
exceptional. . . . . excepcional
existential . . . . existencial
experimental. . . . . experimental
exponential. . . . . exponencial
extramarital . . . . extramatrimonial

facial . . . . facial
factual . . . . factual
fatal. . . . . fatal *(also used for "terrible," "lousy")*
federal . . . . federal
festival . . . . festival
fetal. . . . . fetal
feudal . . . . feudal
filial. . . . . filial
final. . . . . **final**
fiscal . . . . fiscal
floral . . . . floral

focal . . . . focal
formal . . . . formal
fraternal . . . . fraternal
frontal . . . . frontal
frugal . . . . frugal
functional . . . . funcional
fundamental . . . . **fundamental**
funeral . . . . funeral

gastrointestinal . . . . gastrointestinal
general . . . . **general**
generational . . . . generacional
genial . . . . genial *(meaning "talented," "brilliant")*
germinal . . . . germinal
glacial . . . . glacial
global . . . . global
gradual . . . . gradual
grammatical . . . . gramatical
gravitational . . . . gravitacional
guttural . . . . gutural

habitual . . . . habitual
heterosexual . . . . heterosexual
homosexual . . . . homosexual
horizontal . . . . horizontal
hormonal . . . . hormonal
hospital . . . . **hospital**

ideal . . . . **ideal**
illegal . . . . **ilegal**
    "Stealing is illegal." . . . . **"Robar es ilegal".**
immaterial . . . . inmaterial
immoral . . . . inmoral
immortal . . . . inmortal
impartial . . . . imparcial
imperial . . . . imperial

impersonal	impersonal
inaugural	inaugural
incidental	incidental
individual	individual *(adjective only;*
	noun is "individuo")
industrial	industrial
infernal	infernal
informal	informal
initial	**inicial**
institutional	institucional
instrumental	instrumental
insubstantial	insustancial
integral	integral
intellectual	intelectual
intentional.	intencional
intercontinental	intercontinental
international	**internacional**
"It's an international	**"Es una compañía**
company."	**internacional".**
interpersonal.	interpersonal
interracial.	interracial
intestinal.	intestinal
irrational	irracional
jovial	jovial
judicial.	judicial
labial.	labial
lateral	lateral
latitudinal	latitudinal
legal	**legal**
lethal	letal
liberal	liberal
literal	literal

INSTANT Spanish Vocabulary Builder

local . . . . local *(also used as "commercial premises")*

longitudinal. . . . . longitudinal

loyal . . . . leal

manual. . . . . manual

marginal. . . . . marginal

marital . . . . marital

martial . . . . marcial

material . . . . material

maternal. . . . . maternal

matriarchal . . . . matriarcal

matrimonial . . . . matrimonial

medicinal . . . . medicinal

medieval . . . . medieval

menstrual . . . . menstrual

mental . . . . **mental**

"It's a mental problem." . . . . . **"Es un problema mental".**

meridional . . . . meridional *(meaning "Southern")*

metal . . . . metal

mineral. . . . . mineral

modal . . . . modal

monumental . . . . monumental

moral . . . . moral

mortal . . . . mortal

multicultural . . . . multicultural

multifunctional. . . . . multifuncional

multinational . . . . multinacional

municipal . . . . municipal

mural . . . . mural

musical. . . . . musical

mutual . . . . mutual *(more commonly "mutuo")*

nasal . . . . nasal

natal . . . . natal

national	**nacional**
natural	natural
naval	naval
Neanderthal	neandertal
neutral	neutral
nominal	nominal
normal	normal
numeral	numeral
nuptial	nupcial
nutritional	nutricional
occasional	ocasional *(also used for "accidental")*
occidental	occidental *(meaning "Western")*
occupational	ocupacional
octagonal	octagonal
official	oficial
operational	operacional
optional	opcional
oral	oral
ordinal	ordinal
organizational	organizacional
oriental	oriental *(meaning "Eastern")*
original	**original**
ornamental	ornamental
oval	oval
papal	papal
paranormal	paranormal
parochial	parroquial
partial	parcial
pastoral	pastoral
patrimonial	patrimonial
pectoral	pectoral
pedal	pedal
pedestal	pedestal
penal	penal

INSTANT Spanish Vocabulary Builder

personal	personal
phenomenal	fenomenal
plural	plural
portal	portal
positional	posicional
postal	postal
postnatal	postnatal
potential	potencial
preferential	preferencial
prenatal	prenatal
prenuptial	prenupcial
prepositional	preposicional
presidential	presidencial
primordial	primordial
principal	**principal**
procedural	procedimental
processional	procesional
professional	profesional
promotional	promocional
proportional	proporcional
proverbial	proverbial
providential	providencial
provincial	provincial
provisional	provisional
punctual	puntual
racial	racial
radial	radial
radical	radical
rational	racional
real	real
recital	recital
regional	**regional**
relational	relacional
residential	residencial
residual	residual

reverential	reverencial
ritual	ritual
rival	rival
royal	real
rural	rural
sacramental	sacramental
sacrificial	sacrificial
sculptural	escultural
semifinal	semifinal
seminal	seminal
senatorial	senatorial
sensational	sensacional
sensual	sensual
sentimental	sentimental
sepulchral	sepulcral
sequential	secuencial
sexual	sexual
signal	señal
social	**social**
sociocultural	sociocultural
spatial	espacial
special	**especial**
spinal	espinal
spiral	espiral
spiritual	espiritual
structural	estructural
subliminal	subliminal
substantial	sustancial
subtotal	subtotal
subtropical	subtropical
superficial	superficial
supernatural	supernatural
surreal	surreal
tangential	tangencial

INSTANT Spanish Vocabulary Builder

temperamental . . . . temperamental

temporal. . . . . temporal *(also used for "temporary" and "storm")*

terminal . . . . terminal

territorial . . . . territorial

testimonial . . . . testimonial

textual . . . . textual

thermal. . . . . termal *(meaning "related to springs")*

tonal . . . . tonal

torrential. . . . . torrencial

total. . . . . **total**

traditional. . . . . tradicional

transcendental. . . . . trascendental

transcontinental . . . . transcontinental

transitional . . . . transicional

transsexual . . . . transexual

tribal . . . . tribal

tribunal . . . . tribunal *(meaning "courthouse")*

trivial . . . . trivial

tropical. . . . . **tropical**

unconditional . . . . incondicional

unconstitutional . . . . inconstitucional

unequal . . . . desigual

unilateral . . . . unilateral

universal. . . . . universal

unofficial . . . . extraoficial

unreal . . . . irreal

unusual . . . . inusual

urinal. . . . . orinal

usual . . . . usual

vegetal. . . . . vegetal

venal . . . . venal

verbal . . . . verbal

vertical . . . . vertical
vice-presidential . . . . vicepresidencial
viral . . . . viral
virtual . . . . virtual
visceral . . . . visceral
visual . . . . visual
vital . . . . vital
vocal . . . . vocal *(also a noun, "vowel")*
vocational . . . . vocacional

zonal . . . . zonal

Match associated words and/or synonyms.

Una las palabras que están relacionadas o que son sinónimos.

1. animal	contrato
2. personal	gato
3. artificial	sintético
4. crucial	perfecto
5. ideal	importante
6. legal	privado
7. final	terminar

Listen to and read the story. Answer the following questions in complete sentences.

Escuche y lea el cuento. Responda las siguientes preguntas, usando oraciones completas.

(This chapter presents the first story of the travels of Juan and Angélica. Every chapter will feature a new story about these two young Spaniards traveling through Spain. Please listen to and read each story carefully before answering the questions that follow.)

Juan y Angélica son dos jóvenes de Bilbao; ellos quieren hacer un viaje (take a trip)**. Hay un problema—Juan quiere hacer un viaje <u>internacional</u> y Angélica quiere hacer un viaje <u>nacional</u>. Juan dice, "Pero Angélica, tu idea no es <u>original</u>". Angélica dice, "¡Vamos, Juan, no ahora** (not now)**!" Al final, Angélica gana; Juan decide que no es <u>esencial</u> hacer un viaje <u>internacional</u> ahora. Angélica tiene algunas ideas <u>generales</u> para su itinerario. Juan dice, "No quiero visitar a tu tío en**

Córdoba. ¡Él es demasiado <u>formal</u> y <u>tradicional</u>!" Angélica
dice, "Veremos…(we'll see)".

1. ¿De dónde son Juan y Angélica?

2. ¿Qué tipo de viaje quiere hacer Juan?

3. ¿Qué tipo de viaje quiere hacer Angélica?

4. ¿Qué dice Juan de la idea de Angélica?

5. ¿Según Juan (according to Juan), cómo es el tío de Angélica?

Many English words ending in "–ance" correspond to "–ancia" in Spanish.

Spanish words ending in "–ancia" are usually feminine nouns. For example,

distance = *la distancia*

ENGLISH . . . . SPANISH

*All words and phrases in bold are on **Track 2** of the accompanying CD.*

abundance . . . . abundancia
ambulance . . . . **ambulancia**
arrogance . . . . **arrogancia**
    "Nobody likes arrogance." . . . **"A nadie le gusta la arrogancia".**
assistance . . . . asistencia

circumstance . . . . circunstancia
clairvoyance . . . . clarividencia
concordance . . . . concordancia
consonance . . . . consonancia
constance . . . . constancia

discordance . . . . discordancia
dissonance . . . . disonancia
distance . . . . **distancia**

elegance . . . . **elegancia**
extravagance . . . . extravagancia
exuberance . . . . exuberancia

flagrance . . . . flagrancia

fragrance . . . . fragancia
France . . . . Francia

ignorance . . . . ignorancia
importance . . . . **importancia**
    "What is the importance?" . . . **"¿Cuál es la importancia?"**
inobservance . . . . inobservancia
insignificance . . . . insignificancia
instance . . . . instancia
intemperance . . . . intemperancia
intolerance . . . . **intolerancia**
irrelevance . . . . irrelevancia

militance . . . . militancia

observance . . . . observancia

perseverance . . . . **perseverancia**
    "Perseverance is important." . . . **"La perseverancia es importante".**
predominance . . . . predominancia
preponderance . . . . preponderancia
protuberance . . . . protuberancia

redundance . . . . redundancia
relevance . . . . relevancia
repugnance . . . . repugnancia
resistance . . . . resistencia
resonance . . . . resonancia

substance . . . . **substancia**

temperance . . . . temperancia
tolerance . . . . **tolerancia**

variance . . . . variancia
vigilance . . . . vigilancia

2A.

Una las palabras que están relacionadas o que son sinónimos.

1. fragancia	hospital
2. distancia	significado
3. perseverancia	soberbia
4. tolerancia	lejos
5. arrogancia	constancia
6. ambulancia	perfume
7. importancia	paciencia

2B.

Escuche y lea el cuento. Responda las siguientes preguntas, usando oraciones completas.

Para organizar su viaje, Juan y Angélica hablan de muchas cosas. Juan habla de la <u>importancia</u> de no gastar (spend) **mucho; de hecho, Juan no tiene mucha <u>tolerancia</u> hacia el mundo "chic". El sabe que hay gran <u>distancia</u> que cubrir, y que la <u>perseverancia</u> será necesaria. Angélica también entiende la <u>importancia</u> de no gastar mucho dinero durante el viaje. Ella pide** (asks for) **solamente una cosa: quiere ver un baile profesional** (a professional dance) **en Valencia. Una amiga le dijo que es un espectáculo de una <u>elegancia</u> increíble. Juan dice, "Veremos...".**

1. ¿Juan habla de la importancia de qué cosa?

2. ¿Juan no tiene mucha tolerancia hacia qué?

3. ¿Qué será necesario?

4. ¿ Angélica entiende la importancia de no gastar mucho dinero?

5. ¿Cómo responde Juan al pedido (request) de Angélica?

-ant/-ante

English words ending in "–ant" generally correspond to "–ante" in Spanish.

Spanish words ending in "–ante" are usually adjectives or nouns. For example,

arrogant (adj.) = *arrogante*
deodorant (n.) = *el desodorante*

ENGLISH . . . . SPANISH

*All words and phrases in bold are on **Track 3** of the accompanying CD.*

aberrant . . . . aberrante
abundant . . . . **abundante**
ambulant . . . . ambulante
antioxidant . . . . antioxidante
arrogant . . . . **arrogante**
    "He is very arrogant." . . . . . . **"Él es muy arrogante".**
aspirant . . . . aspirante
assailant . . . . asaltante

brilliant . . . . brillante

colorant . . . . colorante
commandant . . . . comandante
communicant . . . . comunicante
concordant . . . . concordante
consonant . . . . consonante
constant . . . . **constante** *(also used for "consistent")*
consultant . . . . consultante
contaminant . . . . contaminante

debutant . . . . debutante

deodorant. . . . . **desodorante**
determinant . . . . determinante
discordant . . . . discordante
disinfectant . . . . desinfectante
dissonant . . . . disonante
distant . . . . distante
dominant . . . . dominante

elegant. . . . . **elegante**
elephant. . . . . **elefante**
emigrant. . . . . emigrante
entrant . . . . entrante
equidistant . . . . equidistante
errant. . . . . errante
exorbitant. . . . . exorbitante
expectant . . . . expectante
extravagant . . . . extravagante *(also used for "odd")*
exuberant. . . . . exuberante
exultant . . . . exultante

flagellant . . . . flagelante
flagrant . . . . flagrante
fluctuant . . . . fluctuante
fumigant. . . . . fumigante

gallant . . . . galante
giant . . . . gigante

ignorant . . . . **ignorante**
    "What an ignorant question!" . . **"¡Qué pregunta tan ignorante!"**
immigrant. . . . . **inmigrante**
implant. . . . . implante
important . . . . **importante**
incessant . . . . incesante
inconstant. . . . . inconstante
indignant . . . . indignante

infant	infante
informant	informante
inhabitant	habitante
inobservant	inobservante
insignificant	insignificante
instant	**instante**
intolerant	intolerante
irrelevant	irrelevante
irritant	irritante
itinerant	itinerante
lubricant	lubricante
merchant	mercante *(only used as an adjective)*
migrant	emigrante
militant	militante
mutant	mutante
observant	observante *(more commonly "observador")*
occupant	**ocupante**
operant	operante
palpitant	palpitante
participant	**participante**
pedant	pedante
piquant	picante
predominant	predominante
preponderant	preponderante
Protestant	protestante
radiant	radiante
rampant	rampante
recalcitrant	recalcitrante
redundant	redundante
refrigerant	refrigerante

relaxant . . . . relajante
relevant . . . . relevante
repugnant. . . . . repugnante
resonant . . . . resonante
restaurant. . . . . **restaurante**
    "That restaurant is cheap." . . . **"Ese restaurante es barato".**

stimulant . . . . **estimulante** *(also used for "stimulating")*
supplicant. . . . . suplicante

tolerant. . . . . tolerante
transplant . . . . transplante
triumphant . . . . **triunfante**

vacant . . . . vacante
variant . . . . variante
vibrant . . . . vibrante
vigilant. . . . . vigilante

3A.

Una las palabras que están relacionadas o que son sinónimos.

1. ignorante   evidente
2. elegante   animal
3. importante   pretencioso
4. elefante   cafetería
5. arrogante   esencial
6. flagrante   desconocedor
7. restaurante   fino

3B.

Escuche y lea el cuento. Responda las siguientes preguntas, usando oraciones completas.

Juan y Angélica deciden ir primero a una ciudad <u>importante</u>: ¡Barcelona! Angélica dice, "Pero Juan, ¿es verdad que la gente (the people) **de Barcelona es <u>arrogante</u>?" Juan responde, "¡Pero qué pregunta tan <u>ignorante</u>! No, la gente de Barcelona no es <u>arrogante</u>, su modo de vestir** (way of dressing) **es muy <u>elegante</u> y saben que la historia de Barcelona es muy <u>importante</u>, pero... son personas muy simpáticas". Juan tiene un amigo, Andrés, que vive en Barcelona y tiene un <u>restaurante</u> que se llama El <u>Elefante</u> Rojo. Apenas llegan** (as soon as they arrive) **a Barcelona, van a comer al <u>restaurante</u> de Andrés. Él les sirve una cena <u>abundante</u>.**

1. ¿A qué ciudad van Juan y Angélica?

2. ¿Qué piensa Angélica de la gente de Barcelona?

3. ¿Qué dice Juan del modo de vestir de la gente de Barcelona?

4. ¿Cómo describe Juan la historia de Barcelona?

5. ¿Cómo se llama el restaurante de Andrés?

 **-ar/-ar**

Many English words ending in "–ar" have the same ending in Spanish.

Spanish words ending in "–ar" are usually verbs, nouns, or adjectives. For example,

> to arrive (v.) = *llegar*   a dollar (n.) = *un dólar*
> spectacular (adj.) = *espectacular*

ENGLISH . . . . SPANISH

All words and phrases in bold are on **Track 4** *of the accompanying CD.*

altar. . . . . altar
angular . . . . angular
antinuclear . . . . antinuclear
bipolar. . . . . bipolar
Caesar. . . . . César
cardiovascular . . . . cardiovascular
caviar . . . . caviar
cellular. . . . . **celular**
    "It's a cellular phone." . . . . . . **"Es un teléfono celular".**
circular. . . . . **circular**
    "It has a circular shape." . . . . **"Tiene una forma circular".**
collar . . . . collar *(meaning "necklace")*
curricular . . . . curricular

dollar. . . . . dólar

electronuclear . . . . electronuclear
exemplar . . . . ejemplar
extracurricular. . . . . extracurricular

familiar . . . . familiar

glandular . . . . glandular
globular . . . . globular
granular . . . . granular

insular . . . . insular
intramuscular . . . . intramuscular
irregular . . . . irregular

jugular . . . . yugular

lunar . . . . lunar *(also used for "mole")*

modular . . . . modular
molecular . . . . molecular
multicellular . . . . multicelular
muscular . . . . muscular *(only used for "of the muscle")*

nectar . . . . néctar
nuclear . . . . **nuclear**
    "Nuclear war is terrible." . . . . **"La guerra nuclear es terrible".**

ocular . . . . ocular

particular . . . . particular
peculiar . . . . peculiar
peninsular . . . . peninsular
perpendicular . . . . perpendicular
polar . . . . **polar**
popular . . . . **popular** *(also used for "of the people")*

radar . . . . radar
rectangular . . . . rectangular
regular . . . . regular *(also used for "less than good")*

scholar . . . . escolar *(meaning "pupil,"*
or "of the school")

secular . . . . secular

semicircular . . . . semicircular

similar . . . . similar

singular . . . . singular

solar . . . . solar

spectacular . . . . **espectacular**

stellar . . . . estelar

subpolar . . . . subpolar

sugar . . . . azúcar

thermonuclear . . . . termonuclear

triangular . . . . triangular

tubular . . . . tubular

tzar . . . . zar

unicellular . . . . unicelular

unpopular . . . . impopular

vascular . . . . vascular

vehicular . . . . vehicular

vulgar . . . . **vulgar**

4A.

Una las palabras que están relacionadas o que son sinónimos.

1. cardiovascular	corazón
2. regular	moneda
3. singular	atómico
4. circular	parecido
5. similar	redondo
6. dólar	constante
7. nuclear	único

4B.

Escuche y lea el cuento. Responda las siguientes preguntas, usando oraciones completas.

Mientras están en (while in) **Barcelona, Juan y Angélica van a una lección de italiano con Andrés, el amigo de Juan. Angélica pregunta, "¿Por qué tienes un interés tan <u>particular</u> por el italiano?" Andrés responde, "Porque el italiano es muy <u>popular</u> en Ibiza, y quiero trabajar** (I want to work) **en Ibiza". Durante la lección, el profesor habla de muchos verbos <u>irregulares</u>. Después de la lección, los tres amigos hablan de la diferencia entre** (between) **el <u>singular</u> y el plural en el italiano. El italiano es muy difícil para Angélica. Ella dice, "¡Nada es <u>regular</u>, todo es <u>irregular</u>! ¡Para mí, el italiano es muy difícil!"**

1. ¿Adónde van mientras están en Barcelona?

2. ¿Por qué estudia Andrés italiano?

3. ¿De qué habla el profesor?

4. ¿Los tres amigos hablan de la diferencia entre qué cosas?

5. ¿Angélica piensa que el italiano es muy regular?

INSTANT Spanish Vocabulary Builder

-ary/-ario

Many English words ending in "–ary" correspond to "–ario" in Spanish.

Spanish words ending in "–ario" are usually masculine nouns or adjectives. For example,

> anniversary (n.) = *un aniversario*
> ordinary (adj.) = *ordinario*

ENGLISH . . . . SPANISH

All words and phrases in bold are on **Track 5** *of the accompanying CD.*

actuary . . . . actuario
adversary . . . . adversario
anniversary . . . . **aniversario**
antiquary . . . . anticuario
arbitrary . . . . arbitrario

beneficiary . . . . beneficiario
bestiary . . . . bestiario
binary . . . . binario
breviary . . . . breviario

canary . . . . canario
centenary . . . . centenario
commentary . . . . comentario *(also used for "comment")*
commissary. . . . . comisario
complementary . . . . complementario
contrary . . . . **contrario**
corollary. . . . . corolario
coronary . . . . coronario
culinary . . . . culinario

depositary . . . . depositario
diary . . . . diario *(also used for "newspaper")*
dictionary . . . . **diccionario**
    "He is using the dictionary.". . . **"El está usando el diccionario".**
dignitary . . . . dignatario
disciplinary . . . . disciplinario
dispensary . . . . dispensario
divisionary . . . . divisionario
documentary . . . . documentario *(more commonly "documental," as a noun)*

emissary . . . . emisario
estuary . . . . estuario
extraordinary . . . . **extraordinario**

fiduciary . . . . fiduciario
fragmentary . . . . fragmentario
functionary . . . . funcionario
funerary . . . . funerario

glossary . . . . **glosario**

hereditary . . . . hereditario
honorary . . . . honorario

imaginary . . . . **imaginario**
    "He has an imaginary friend." . . . **"Él tiene un amigo imaginario".**
incendiary . . . . incendiario
interdisciplinary . . . . interdisciplinario
intermediary . . . . intermediario
involuntary . . . . involuntario
itinerary . . . . **itinerario**

lapidary . . . . lapidario
legendary . . . . legendario
literary . . . . literario

mercenary . . . . mercenario
monetary . . . . monetario

necessary . . . . **necesario**
notary . . . . notario

obituary . . . . obituario
ordinary . . . . **ordinario**
ovary . . . . ovario

parliamentary . . . . parlamentario
penitentiary . . . . penitenciario
planetary . . . . planetario
plenary . . . . plenario
primary . . . . primario
proprietary . . . . propietario (also used for "owner")

questionary . . . . cuestionario (meaning "questionnaire")

reactionary . . . . reaccionario
revolutionary . . . . **revolucionario**
rosary . . . . rosario
rudimentary . . . . rudimentario

salary . . . . **salario**
   "You have a good salary." . . . **"Tú tienes un buen salario".**
sanctuary . . . . santuario
sanitary . . . . sanitario
secondary . . . . secundario
secretary . . . . **secretario** (more commonly used in
                                       feminine form, "secretaria")
sedentary . . . . sedentario
sedimentary . . . . sedimentario
seminary . . . . seminario
solitary . . . . **solitario**
stationary . . . . estacionario

subsidiary. . . . . subsidiario

summary . . . . sumario

supplementary. . . . . suplementario

temporary. . . . . temporario

tertiary . . . . terciario

tributary . . . . tributario

unitary . . . . unitario

unnecessary . . . . innecesario

urinary. . . . . urinario

veterinary. . . . . veterinario

visionary . . . . visionario

vocabulary . . . . **vocabulario** *(also used for "dictionary")*

   "Vocabulary is important." . . . **"El vocabulario es importante".**

voluntary . . . . voluntario *(also used for "volunteer")*

5A.

Una las palabras que están relacionadas o que son sinónimos.

1. aniversario	palabras
2. salario	ruta
3. necesario	común
4. vocabulario	cumpleaños
5. itinerario	opuesto
6. ordinario	vital
7. contrario	dinero

5B.

Escuche y lea el cuento. Responda las siguientes preguntas, usando oraciones completas.

Juan y Angélica tienen un <u>itinerario</u> muy intenso en Barcelona. Para no olvidar (to not forget) **su aventura, Angélica quiere comprar un <u>diario</u> para escribir todo. Un día van a las Ramblas, otro día van a la Sagrada Familia, otro día van a Montserrat. Juan dice, "¡Este ritmo** (this pace) **es <u>extraordinario</u>!" Cada noche, Angélica escribe mucho en su <u>diario</u>, pero Juan no comprende. El dice, "No es <u>necesario</u> escribir cada detalle** (every detail)**—¡no es un <u>diccionario</u>!" Angélica responde, "Al <u>contrario</u>, ¡es muy importante escribir cada detalle!"**

1. ¿Cómo es el itinerario de Juan y Angélica en Barcelona?

2. ¿Qué quiere comprar Angélica?

3. ¿Qué escribe Angélica en su diario?

4. ¿Qué dice Juan del ritmo?

5. ¿Según Juan, no es necesario hacer qué cosa?

-ble/-ble

Many English words ending in "–ble" have the same ending in Spanish.

Spanish words ending in "–ble" are usually adjectives. For example,

a <u>flexible</u> schedule = *un horario <u>flexible</u>*

ENGLISH . . . . SPANISH

*All words and phrases in bold are on **Track 6** of the accompanying CD.*

English	Spanish
abominable	abominable
acceptable	**aceptable**
accessible	accesible *(also used for "approachable")*
accusable	acusable
adaptable	adaptable
adjustable	ajustable
admirable	admirable
admissible	admisible
adoptable	adoptable
adorable	**adorable**
"The baby is adorable."	**"El bebé es adorable".**
affable	afable
agreeable	agradable
alienable	alienable
alterable	alterable
amiable	amable
amicable	amigable
appealable	apelable
applicable	aplicable
appreciable	apreciable
arable	arable
audible	audible

biodegradable . . . . biodegradable

cable . . . . cable
calculable. . . . . calculable
cancelable . . . . cancelable
censurable . . . . censurable
classifiable . . . . clasificable
coercible . . . . coercible
collectible. . . . . coleccionable
combinable. . . . . combinable
combustible . . . . combustible
comfortable . . . . confortable *(more commonly "cómodo")*
commemorable . . . . conmemorable
commensurable . . . . conmensurable
communicable. . . . . comunicable
commutable . . . . conmutable
comparable . . . . **comparable**
compatible . . . . compatible
comprehensible. . . . . comprensible
computable. . . . . computable
condemnable . . . . condenable
condensable . . . . condensable
condonable . . . . condonable
confessable. . . . . confesable
conservable . . . . conservable
considerable. . . . . considerable
consolable . . . . consolable
consumable . . . . consumible
contestable . . . . contestable
controllable. . . . . controlable
controvertible . . . . controvertible
convertible . . . . convertible
corruptible . . . . corruptible
countable . . . . contable (also used for "accountant")
credible . . . . **creíble**
    "His story is not credible." . . . **"Su cuento no es creíble".**

criticizable . . . . criticable
culpable . . . . culpable
curable . . . . curable

deductible . . . . deducible
defensible . . . . defendible
definable . . . . definible
degradable . . . . degradable
delectable . . . . deleitable
demonstrable . . . . demostrable
deplorable . . . . deplorable
describable . . . . descriptible
desirable . . . . deseable
destructible . . . . destructible
determinable . . . . determinable
detestable . . . . detestable
digestible . . . . digerible
discussible . . . . discutible
disposable . . . . disponible *(meaning "available")*
disputable . . . . disputable
distillable . . . . destilable
divisible . . . . **divisible**
dubitable . . . . dudable
durable . . . . durable *(more commonly "duradero")*

eligible . . . . elegible
eliminable . . . . eliminable
emendable . . . . enmendable
enviable . . . . envidiable
estimable . . . . estimable
evaporable . . . . evaporable
evitable . . . . evitable
excitable . . . . excitable
excludible . . . . excluible
excusable . . . . **excusable**
expansible . . . . expansible

explicable. . . . . explicable
explorable . . . . explorable
exportable . . . . exportable
extensible . . . . extensible

fallible . . . . falible
favorable . . . . favorable
fermentable. . . . . fermentable
filmable . . . . filmable
flexible. . . . . **flexible**
formidable . . . . formidable *(also used for "great,"*
"super")

governable. . . . . gobernable

habitable . . . . habitable
honorable. . . . . honorable
horrible . . . . **horrible**

identifiable . . . . identificable
ignoble . . . . innoble
illegible . . . . ilegible
imaginable. . . . . imaginable
imitable . . . . imitable
impassible . . . . impasible
impeccable . . . . **impecable**
    "Your Spanish is impeccable.". . . **"Tu español es impecable".**
impenetrable. . . . . impenetrable
imperceptible . . . . imperceptible
impermeable. . . . . impermeable *(also used for "raincoat")*
imperturbable . . . . imperturbable
implacable . . . . implacable
impossible . . . . **imposible**
impressionable . . . . impresionable
improbable. . . . . **improbable**
inaccessible . . . . inaccesible

inadmissible . . . . inadmisible

inalienable . . . . inalienable

inapplicable . . . . inaplicable

inappreciable . . . . inapreciable *(meaning "invaluable")*

inaudible . . . . inaudible

incalculable . . . . incalculable

incomparable . . . . incomparable

incompatible . . . . incompatible

incomprehensible . . . . incomprensible

inconsolable . . . . inconsolable

incontestable . . . . incontestable

incontrovertible . . . . incontrovertible

incorrigible . . . . incorregible

incorruptible . . . . incorruptible

incredible . . . . **increíble**

incurable . . . . incurable

indefatigable . . . . infatigable

indefinable . . . . indefinible

indelible . . . . indeleble

indescribable . . . . indescriptible

indestructible . . . . indestructible

indigestible . . . . indigerible

indispensable . . . . indispensable

indivisible . . . . indivisible

ineffable . . . . inefable

ineligible . . . . inelegible

inestimable . . . . inestimable

inevitable . . . . **inevitable**

inexcusable . . . . inexcusable

inexorable . . . . inexorable

inexplicable . . . . inexplicable

inextricable . . . . inextricable

infallible . . . . infalible

inflammable . . . . inflamable

inflexible . . . . **inflexible**

inhabitable . . . . habitable

inimitable	inimitable
inoperable	inoperable
insatiable	insaciable
inscrutable	inescrutable
insensible	insensible *(meaning "insensitive")*
inseparable	inseparable
insoluble	insoluble
insuperable	insuperable
intangible	intangible
intelligible	inteligible
interminable	interminable
interpretable	interpretable
intolerable	intolerable
invariable	invariable
invertible	invertible *(meaning "investable")*
invincible	invencible
inviolable	inviolable
invisible	**invisible**

"The cover is invisible." . . . . . **"La tapa es invisible".**

invulnerable	invulnerable
irascible	irascible
irreconcilable	irreconciliable
irreducible	irreducible *(also used for "unyielding")*
irrefutable	irrefutable
irresistible	irresistible
irresponsible	**irresponsable**
irreversible	irreversible
irrevocable	irrevocable
irrigable	irrigable
irritable	irritable
lamentable	lamentable
laudable	laudable
legible	legible
limitable	limitable

INSTANT Spanish Vocabulary Builder

malleable . . . . maleable

manageable . . . . manejable

maneuverable . . . . maniobrable

measurable . . . . mensurable

memorable . . . . memorable

miserable . . . . **miserable** *(also used for "greedy,"*
or "evil")

modifiable . . . . modificable

multipliable . . . . multiplicable

navigable . . . . navegable

negotiable . . . . negociable

noble . . . . **noble**

notable . . . . notable

observable . . . . observable

operable . . . . operable

ostensible . . . . ostensible

palpable . . . . palpable

pardonable . . . . perdonable

passable . . . . **pasable**

"The wine is passable (so-so)." . . . **"El vino está pasable nada más".**

payable . . . . pagable

penetrable . . . . penetrable

perceptible . . . . perceptible

perfectible . . . . perfectible

permeable . . . . permeable

permissible . . . . permisible

persuadable . . . . persuasible

placable . . . . aplacable

plausible . . . . plausible

ponderable . . . . ponderable

possible . . . . **posible**

potable . . . . potable

preferable . . . . preferible

presentable.	presentable
probable	**probable**
producible	producible
programmable	programable
provable.	probable
publishable.	publicable
qualifiable	calificable
quantifiable	cuantificable
realizable.	realizable
recommendable	recomendable
reconcilable	reconciliable
recyclable.	reciclable
reducible	reducible
reformable	reformable
refutable.	refutable
renewable	renovable
repairable	**reparable**
repeatable	repetible
replicable.	replicable
reprehensible	reprensible
representable	representable
resistible.	resistible
respectable.	**respetable**

"She's a respectable lady." . . . **"Es una señora respetable".**

responsible.	**responsable**
restorable.	restaurable
retractable	retractable
reversible	reversible
revocable	revocable
savable	salvable
sensible	sensible *(meaning "sensitive")*
separable.	separable
sociable	sociable

INSTANT Spanish Vocabulary Builder

soluble . . . . soluble
stable . . . . **estable** *(only an
adjective; "horse stable" is* "establo")
superable . . . . superable
susceptible . . . . susceptible

tangible . . . . tangible
terminable . . . . terminable
terrible . . . . terrible
tolerable . . . . tolerable
touchable . . . . tocable
transferable . . . . transferible
transformable . . . . transformable

unacceptable . . . . inaceptable
unadaptable . . . . inadaptable
unalterable . . . . inalterable
unclassifiable . . . . inclasificable
uncontrollable . . . . incontrolable
undesirable . . . . indeseable
undeterminable . . . . indeterminable
undisputable . . . . indisputable
unimaginable . . . . inimaginable
unintelligible . . . . ininteligible
unsociable . . . . insociable
unstable . . . . inestable
untouchable . . . . intocable
utilizable . . . . utilizable

variable . . . . **variable**
venerable . . . . venerable
verifiable . . . . verificable
viable . . . . viable
visible . . . . **visible**
vulnerable . . . . vulnerable

6A.

Una las palabras que están relacionadas o que son sinónimos.

1. flexible	rígido
2. terrible	bonito
3. probable	seguro
4. estable	posible
5. inflexible	infeliz
6. miserable	elástico
7. adorable	horrible

6B.

Escuche y lea el cuento. Responda las siguientes preguntas, usando oraciones completas.

Después de unos días en Barcelona, Juan y Angélica toman el tren a Valencia. Durante el viaje en tren tienen una pelea (an argument). **Angélica le dice a Juan, "¡Tú eres muy <u>irresponsable</u>! ¡No reservaste** (you didn't reserve) **los asientos para el baile!" Juan responde, "¡Tú eres <u>inflexible</u>, podemos ir en otra ocasión; es muy <u>probable</u> que regresemos a Valencia algún día!" Angélica dice, "¡Eres <u>imposible</u>! ¡Es bastante <u>improbable</u> que regresemos a Valencia!" Al final Juan pide disculpas** (apologizes) **y dice que será mucho más <u>responsable</u> durante el resto del viaje. Angélica pregunta si será <u>posible</u> comprar los boletos para el baile en Valencia. Juan responde, "Veremos…".**

1. ¿Adónde van después de Barcelona?

2. ¿Qué piensa Angélica de Juan?

3. ¿Qué dice Juan de Angélica?

4. ¿Angélica piensa que es probable que regresen a Valencia algún día?

5. ¿Qué pregunta Angélica al final?

-ct/-cto

English words ending in "–ct" often correspond to "–cto" in Spanish.

Spanish words ending in "–cto" are usually masculine nouns or adjectives. For example,

> contact (n.) = *un contacto*
> direct (adj.) = *directo*

ENGLISH . . . . SPANISH

All words and phrases in bold are on **Track 7** *of the accompanying CD.*

abstract . . . . abstracto
act. . . . . acto
addict . . . . adicto
adjunct. . . . . adjunto
affect . . . . afecto
aqueduct . . . . acueducto
architect. . . . . arquitecto
artifact . . . . artefacto
aspect . . . . **aspecto**

circumspect. . . . . circunspecto
compact. . . . . compacto
conflict . . . . conflicto
contact . . . . **contacto**
contract . . . . **contrato**
    "The new contract is better." . . . **"El contrato nuevo es mejor"**.
convict . . . . convicto
correct . . . . **correcto**

defect. . . . . defecto
defunct. . . . . difunto
derelict. . . . . derelicto
dialect . . . . **dialecto**
direct . . . . **directo**
    "It's a direct flight." . . . . **"Es un vuelo directo"**.
distinct . . . . distinto *(meaning "different")*
district . . . . distrito

edict . . . . edicto
effect . . . . efecto
exact . . . . exacto
extinct . . . . extinto
extract . . . . extracto

impact . . . . impacto
imperfect . . . . imperfecto
incorrect. . . . . **incorrecto**
    "The answer is incorrect." . . . **"La respuesta es incorrecta"**.
indirect. . . . . **indirecto**
indistinct. . . . . indistinto
inexact. . . . . inexacto
insect. . . . . insecto
instinct . . . . instinto
intact . . . . intacto
intellect. . . . . intelecto

object . . . . objeto

pact. . . . . pacto
perfect . . . . perfecto
prefect . . . . prefecto
product . . . . producto
project . . . . proyecto
prospect. . . . . prospecto

    INSTANT Spanish Vocabulary Builder

select . . . . selecto *(only an adjective)*   **-ct/-cto**
strict . . . . estricto
succinct . . . . sucinto

tact . . . . tacto

verdict . . . . veredicto
viaduct . . . . viaducto

7A.

Una las palabras que están relacionadas o que son sinónimos.

1. correcto	ideal
2. perfecto	bien
3. incorrecto	parte
4. dialecto	mosca
5. acto	idioma
6. aspecto	mal
7. insecto	teatro

7B.

Escuche y lea el cuento. Responda las siguientes preguntas, usando oraciones completas.

Después de bajar del tren <u>directo</u> de Barcelona a Valencia, Angélica pregunta si éste es el lugar <u>correcto</u> porque ella no comprende nada. Ella sabe que el español hablado (spoken Spanish) no es siempre <u>perfecto</u>, ¡pero no comprende este acento ni un poquito! Juan dice, "No te preocupes (don't worry), tengo un buen <u>contacto</u> aquí en Valencia; se llama Alfonso, y él nos ayudará a conseguir los boletos". Después de unos minutos en la estación, Alfonso viene a recogerlos (pick them up). "Tiene <u>aspecto</u> de ser muy buena persona", dice Angélica. Alfonso es muy gracioso y tiene mucho respeto por su amigo Juan y su novia Angélica. Después de una buena cena en casa de Alfonso—la salsa estuvo <u>perfecta</u>—Angélica le pregunta si sabe algo sobre el baile en el centro. Alfonso responde, "Veremos...".

INSTANT Spanish Vocabulary Builder

1. ¿Qué tipo de tren tomaron de Barcelona?

2. ¿Por qué piensa Angélica que no es el lugar correcto?

3. ¿Por qué no comprende Angélica el español en Valencia?

4. ¿Cómo se llama el contacto de Juan en Valencia?

5. ¿Cómo estuvo la salsa de Alfonso?

-ence/-encia

English words ending in "–ence" often correspond to "–encia" in Spanish.

Spanish words ending in "–encia" are usually feminine nouns. For example,

a difference = *una diferencia*

ENGLISH . . . . SPANISH

*All words and phrases in bold are on **Track 8** of the accompanying CD.*

absence . . . . **ausencia**
abstinence . . . . abstinencia
adherence . . . . adherencia
adolescence . . . . adolescencia
ambivalence . . . . ambivalencia
antiviolence . . . . antiviolencia
audience . . . . audiencia *(more commonly "público")*

belligerence . . . . beligerancia
beneficence . . . . beneficencia
benevolence . . . . benevolencia

cadence . . . . cadencia
circumference . . . . circunferencia
coexistence. . . . . coexistencia
coherence. . . . . coherencia
coincidence. . . . . **coincidencia**
    "What a coincidence!" . . . . . **"¡Qué coincidencia!"**
competence . . . . competencia *(also used for "competition")*
complacence. . . . . complacencia
condescendence . . . . condescendencia

condolence	condolencia
conference	**conferencia**
confidence	confidencia *(meaning "secret/private information")*
confluence	confluencia
congruence	congruencia
conscience	conciencia
consequence	**consecuencia**
consistence	consistencia
continence	continencia
convalescence	convalecencia
convenience	conveniencia
convergence	convergencia
corpulence	corpulencia
correspondence	correspondencia
decadence	decadencia
deference	deferencia
dependence	dependencia
difference	**diferencia**

"The difference is notable." . . . **"La diferencia es notable".**

diligence	diligencia
disobedience	desobediencia
dissidence	disidencia
divergence	divergencia
effervescence	efervescencia
eloquence	elocuencia
emergence	emergencia *(meaning "emergency")*
eminence	eminencia
equivalence	equivalencia
essence	esencia
evidence	evidencia
excellence	excelencia
existence	existencia
experience	**experiencia**

INSTANT Spanish Vocabulary Builder

fluorescence . . . . fluorescencia
frequence . . . . frecuencia *(also used for "frequency")*

imminence . . . . inminencia
impatience . . . . **impaciencia**
impermanence . . . . impermanencia
impertinence . . . . impertinencia
impotence . . . . impotencia
imprudence . . . . imprudencia
impudence . . . . impudencia
incandescence . . . . incandescencia
incidence . . . . incidencia *(also used for "impact," "effect")*

incoherence . . . . incoherencia
incompetence . . . . incompetencia
incongruence . . . . incongruencia
inconsequence . . . . inconsecuencia
inconsistence . . . . inconsistencia
incontinence . . . . incontinencia
inconvenience . . . . inconveniencia
independence . . . . independencia
indifference . . . . **indiferencia**
   "I hate indifference." . . . . **"Odio la indiferencia".**
indigence . . . . indigencia
indolence . . . . indolencia
indulgence . . . . indulgencia
inexistence . . . . inexistencia
inexperience . . . . inexperiencia
inference . . . . inferencia
influence . . . . **influencia**
infrequence . . . . infrecuencia
innocence . . . . **inocencia**
insistence . . . . insistencia
insolence . . . . insolencia
intelligence . . . . **inteligencia**

interdependence . . . . interdependencia
interference. . . . . interferencia
intransigence . . . . intransigencia
irreverence . . . . irreverencia

jurisprudence . . . . jurisprudencia

license . . . . licencia *(also used for "permit")*
luminescence . . . . luminiscencia

magnificence . . . . magnificencia
malevolence . . . . malevolencia
munificence . . . . munificencia

negligence . . . . negligencia
neuroscience. . . . . neurociencia

obedience . . . . obediencia
obsolescence . . . . obsolescencia
occurrence . . . . ocurrencia *(also used for
"bright idea")*
omnipotence. . . . . omnipotencia
omnipresence . . . . omnipresencia
opulence . . . . opulencia

patience . . . . **paciencia**
   "Pedro has little patience." . . . **"Pedro tiene poca paciencia".**
penitence . . . . penitencia
permanence . . . . permanencia
persistence . . . . persistencia
pertinence . . . . pertinencia
pestilence. . . . . pestilencia
precedence. . . . . precedencia
preeminence. . . . . preeminencia
preexistence . . . . preexistencia
preference . . . . **preferencia**

presence. . . . . **presencia**
prominence. . . . . prominencia
providence . . . . providencia
prudence . . . . prudencia

quintessence . . . . quintaesencia

reference . . . . referencia
reminiscence. . . . . reminiscencia
residence . . . . **residencia**
reticence . . . . reticencia
reverence . . . . reverencia

science . . . . **ciencia**
sentence. . . . . sentencia *(meaning "ruling")*
sequence . . . . **secuencia**
somnolence. . . . . somnolencia
subsistence . . . . subsistencia
succulence . . . . suculencia

teleconference. . . . . teleconferencia
transcendence. . . . . transcendencia
transference . . . . transferencia
transparence. . . . . trasparencia
truculence. . . . . truculencia
turbulence. . . . . turbulencia

vehemence . . . . vehemencia
videoconference . . . . videoconferencia
violence . . . . **violencia**
virulence. . . . . virulencia

8A.

Una las palabras que están relacionadas o que son sinónimos.

1. paciencia	prueba
2. conferencia	reunión
3. residencia	guerra
4. diferencia	liberación
5. violencia	casa
6. evidencia	esperar
7. independencia	distinción

8B.

Escuche y lea el cuento. Responda las siguientes preguntas, usando oraciones completas.

El día después, Alfonso le dice a Angélica, "¡Qué <u>coincidencia</u>! Mi novia y yo vamos al baile mañana por la noche, ¿queréis venir (do you two want to come) **con nosotros?" El día después Angélica está muy contenta y le dice a Juan: "¿Ves? La <u>persistencia</u> y <u>diligencia</u> ayudan". Juan está muy contento por la felicidad de Angélica y piensa que será una buena <u>experiencia</u>. Desafortunadamente** (unfortunately) **Juan no tiene ni mucha <u>paciencia</u> ni mucho interés por el baile. Trata de esconder** (he tries to hide) **su <u>indiferencia</u>. Juan le dice a Angélica, "Lo siento por mi <u>impaciencia</u>, pero… ¡el baile está terrible!" Después de dos días con Alfonso en Valencia, Juan y Angélica van a Ibiza.**

1. ¿Qué dice Alfonso del baile?

2. Según Angélica, ¿qué cosas ayudan?

3. ¿Qué expectativas (expectations) tiene Juan hacia el baile?

4. ¿A Juan le causa pasión o indiferencia el baile?

5. ¿Por qué pide disculpas (apologizes) Juan?

English words ending in "–ent" often correspond to "–ente" in Spanish (excluding words ending in "–ment," which is a separate pattern).

Spanish words ending in "–ente" are usually adjectives or nouns. For example,

> innocent (adj.) = *inocente*
> client (n.) = *un/una cliente*

ENGLISH . . . . SPANISH

*All words and phrases in bold are on **Track 9** of the accompanying CD.*

absent . . . . ausente
absorbent . . . . absorbente
accident . . . . accidente
adherent . . . . adherente
adjacent . . . . adyacente
adolescent . . . . adolescente
agent . . . . **agente**
ambient . . . . ambiente *(meaning "environment")*
ambivalent . . . . ambivalente
antecedent . . . . antecedente
apparent . . . . aparente
ardent . . . . ardiente
astringent . . . . astringente

benevolent . . . . benevolente

client . . . . **cliente**
   "Miguel has no clients." . . . . **"Miguel no tiene clientes".**
coefficient . . . . coeficiente

coexistent . . . . coexistente
coherent . . . . coherente
competent . . . . **competente**
complacent . . . . complaciente *(meaning "willing*
to please")

component . . . . componente
concupiscent . . . . concupiscente
concurrent . . . . concurrente
confident . . . . confidente *(meaning "a confidant")*
congruent . . . . congruente
consequent . . . . consiguiente
consistent . . . . consistente *(meaning "firm," "solid")*
constituent . . . . constituyente
continent . . . . **continente**
contingent . . . . contingente
convalescent . . . . convalesciente
convenient . . . . conveniente
convergent . . . . convergente
copresident . . . . copresidente
correspondent . . . . correspondiente
crescent . . . . creciente
current . . . . corriente

decadent . . . . decadente
decent . . . . decente
deficient . . . . deficiente
delinquent . . . . delincuente
dependent . . . . dependiente *(also used for "employee")*
descendent . . . . descendiente
detergent . . . . detergente
different . . . . **diferente**
"I want something different." . . . . **"Quiero algo diferente"**.
diligent . . . . diligente
disobedient . . . . desobediente
dissident . . . . disidente
dissolvent . . . . disolvente

divergent . . . . divergente

effervescent . . . . efervescente
efficient . . . . eficiente
eloquent . . . . elocuente
emergent . . . . emergente
eminent . . . . eminente
equivalent . . . . equivalente
evanescent . . . . evanescente
evident . . . . evidente
excellent . . . . excelente
exigent . . . . exigente
existent . . . . existente
exponent . . . . exponente

fervent . . . . ferviente
fluorescent . . . . fluorescente
frequent . . . . **frecuente**

imminent . . . . inminente
impatient . . . . **impaciente**
    "Carlos is very impatient." . . . **"Carlos es muy impaciente"**.
impertinent . . . . impertinente
impotent . . . . impotente
imprudent . . . . imprudente
impudent . . . . impudente
incandescent . . . . incandescente
incident . . . . incidente
incipient . . . . incipiente
incoherent . . . . incoherente
incompetent . . . . incompetente
incongruent . . . . incongruente
inconsistent . . . . inconsistente *(meaning "flimsy")*
incontinent . . . . incontinente
inconvenient . . . . inconveniente *(also used for*
                                                "inconvenience")

indecent . . . . indecente
independent . . . . independiente
indifferent . . . . **indiferente**
indigent . . . . indigente
indolent . . . . indolente
indulgent . . . . indulgente
inefficient . . . . ineficiente
inexistent . . . . inexistente
infrequent . . . . infrecuente
ingredient . . . . **ingrediente**
inherent . . . . inherente
innocent . . . . **inocente**
insistent . . . . insistente
insolent . . . . insolente
insolvent . . . . insolvente
insufficient . . . . insuficiente
insurgent . . . . insurgente
intelligent . . . . **inteligente**
    "Pablo is very intelligent." . . . **"Pablo es muy inteligente"**.
interdependent . . . . interdependiente
intermittent . . . . intermitente
intransigent . . . . intransigente
iridescent . . . . iridiscente
irreverent . . . . irreverente

latent . . . . latente
luminescent . . . . luminiscente

magnificent . . . . magnificente *(more commonly*
                                    "magnífico")
munificent . . . . munificente

nascent . . . . naciente
negligent . . . . negligente
nutrient . . . . nutriente

obedient	obediente
occident	occidente
omnipotent	omnipotente
omnipresent	omnipresente
omniscient	omnisciente
orient	oriente
parent	pariente *(meaning "a relative")*
patent	patente
patient	**paciente**
penitent	penitente
permanent	**permanente**
persistent	persistente
pertinent	pertinente
pestilent	pestilente
phosphorescent	fosforescente
potent	potente
precedent	precedente
preeminent	preeminente
preexistent	preexistente
present	**presente**
president	**presidente**

"There's a new president." . . . **"Hay un presidente nuevo".**

prominent	prominente
quotient	cociente
recent	reciente
recipient	recipiente *(also used for "container," "bowl")*
recurrent	recurrente
redolent	redolente
repellent	repelente
resident	**residente**
reticent	reticente
reverent	reverente

serpent	serpiente
silent	silente *(more commonly "silencioso")*
solvent	solvente
strident	estridente
subsequent	subsiguiente
sufficient	suficiente
superintendent	superintendente

tangent	**tangente**
torrent	torrente
transcendent	trascendente
transparent	transparente
trident	tridente

urgent	**urgente**

vehement	vehemente
vice president	vicepresidente

9A.

Una las palabras que están relacionadas o que son sinónimos.

1. permanente	obvio
2. reciente	jefe
3. diferente	actual
4. presidente	nuevo
5. evidente	habitante
6. residente	fijo
7. presente	distinto

9B.

Escuche y lea el cuento. Responda las siguientes preguntas, usando oraciones completas.

Cuando llegan a Ibiza, Angélica llama a su madre y recibe un mensaje urgente: debe visitar a su primo (her cousin) **en Ibiza. Su primo Diego es el presidente de una compañía médica. Juan le dice, "Describe a tu primo, ¿cómo es?" Angélica responde, "Bueno, mi primo es... diferente... es un médico muy competente y muy, muy inteligente, pero es un poco extraño** (a bit strange)**". Juan quiere saber por qué es tan "diferente". Angélica le dice, "Ya verás** (you'll see), **él piensa que todos somos médicos residentes". Juan dice, "Está bien, veremos...".**

1. ¿Qué tipo de mensaje recibe Angélica?

2. ¿Diego es el presidente de qué?

3. ¿Qué dice Angélica de su primo?

4. Según Angélica, ¿es Diego inteligente?

5. ¿Qué dice Juan al final?

Chapter 10

Many English words ending in "–gy" correspond to "–gía" in Spanish.

Spanish words ending in "–gía" are usually feminine nouns. For example,

the energy = *la energía*

ENGLISH . . . . SPANISH

All words and phrases in bold are on **Track 10** *of the accompanying CD.*

allergy . . . . **alergia**
    "Ana has a few allergies." . . . **"Ana tiene unas alergias".**
analogy . . . . analogía
anesthesiology . . . . anestesiología
anthology . . . . antología
anthropology . . . . antropología
archaeology . . . . arqueología
astrology . . . . astrología
audiology . . . . audiología

biology . . . . **biología**
biotechnology . . . . biotecnología

cardiology . . . . cardiología
chronology . . . . **cronología**
climatology . . . . climatología
cosmetology . . . . cosmetología
cosmology . . . . cosmología
criminology . . . . criminología
cryptology . . . . criptología

dermatology . . . . dermatología

ecology . . . . ecología
Egyptology . . . . egiptología
elegy . . . . elegía
endocrinology . . . . endocrinología
energy . . . . **energía**
    "We need energy." . . . . **"Necesitamos energía".**
epidemiology . . . . epidemiología
ethnology . . . . etnología
etymology . . . . etimología

gastroenterology . . . . gastroenterología
genealogy . . . . genealogía
geology . . . . **geología**
gynecology . . . . ginecología

hydrology . . . . hidrología

ideology . . . . **ideología**

liturgy . . . . liturgia

meteorology . . . . **meteorología**
methodology . . . . metodología
microbiology . . . . microbiología
mineralogy . . . . mineralogía
morphology . . . . morfología
musicology . . . . musicología
mythology . . . . **mitología**

neurobiology . . . . neurobiología
neurology . . . . neurología
numerology . . . . numerología

oncology . . . . oncología
ontology . . . . ontología
ophthalmology . . . . oftalmología

INSTANT Spanish Vocabulary Builder

orgy. . . . . orgía

paleontology. . . . . paleontología
parapsychology . . . . parasicología
pathology. . . . . patología
pedagogy. . . . . pedagogía
pharmacology. . . . . farmacología
philology . . . . filología
phonology . . . . fonología
phraseology . . . . fraseología
physiology . . . . fisiología
proctology . . . . proctología
psychology . . . . **psicología**
   "She studies psychology." . . . **"Ella estudia psicología"**.

radiology . . . . **radiología**
rheumatology . . . . reumatología

seismology . . . . sismología
sociology . . . . sociología
strategy . . . . **estrategia**
   "They have a strategy." . . . . . **"Ellos tienen una estrategia"**.
synergy . . . . sinergia

technology . . . . **tecnología**
terminology. . . . . terminología
theology. . . . . teología
topology. . . . . topología
toxicology. . . . . toxicología
trilogy . . . . **trilogía**
typology. . . . . tipología

urology . . . . urología

zoology . . . . zoología

10A.

Una las palabras que están relacionadas o que son sinónimos.

1. biología	historia
2. radiología	vida
3. tecnología	tres
4. trilogía	plan
5. estrategia	computadora
6. cronología	rayos X
7. geología	tierra

10B.

Escuche y lea el cuento. Responda las siguientes preguntas, usando oraciones completas.

A las nueve de la mañana Juan y Angélica van a la casa de Diego. Él vive en San Miguel y es un hombre muy simpático y tiene mucha energía. Dice de pronto (suddenly), "Hola muchachos, ¿tienen alguna alergia al café?" Los muchachos dicen que no y todos toman un café juntos. Diego empieza en seguida (right away) a hablar de nuevas tecnologías médicas y le pregunta a Juan si estudia radiología. Juan dice que nunca ha estudiado (he never studied) radiología pero sí hizo un año de biología. Diego le pregunta a Angélica si estudia psicología. Cuando ella dice que no, Diego dice, "Entonces, ¿estudias meteorología?" Angélica mira a Juan; él entiende rapidamente lo que significa "diferente".

INSTANT Spanish Vocabulary Builder

1. ¿Diego es perezoso (lazy) o tiene mucha energía?

2. ¿Los muchachos tienen alergia al café?

3. ¿De qué habla Diego?

4. ¿Estudia Juan radiología?

5. ¿Estudia Angélica psicología?

Chapter 11  -ic/-ico

English words ending in "–ic" often correspond to "–ico" in Spanish.

Spanish words ending in "–ico" are usually adjectives. For example,

a <u>drastic</u> situation = *una situación <u>drástica</u>*

ENGLISH . . . . SPANISH	

All words and phrases in bold are on **Track 11** *of the accompanying CD.*

academic	académico
acoustic	acústico
acrobatic	acrobático
acrylic	acrílico
Adriatic	Adriático
aerobic	aeróbico
aerodynamic.	aerodinámico
aeronautic	aeronáutico
aesthetic.	estético
agnostic	agnóstico
alcoholic.	**alcohólico**
"It's an alcoholic drink.".	**"Es un trago alcohólico"**.
algebraic	algebraico
allergic.	**alérgico**
alphabetic	alfabético
altruistic	altruístico *(more commonly "altruista")*
anabolic.	anabólico
analytic	analítico
anarchic.	anárquico
anatomic	anatómico
anemic.	anémico

anesthetic	anestésico
angelic	angélico *(more commonly "angelical")*
anorexic	anoréxico
antagonistic	antagónico
antarctic	antártico
antibiotic	antibiótico
anticlimactic	anticlimático
antidemocratic	antidemocrático
anti-Semitic	antisemítico
antiseptic	antiséptico
apologetic	apologético
aquatic	acuático
Arabic	arábico *(for language, use "árabe")*
arctic	ártico
archaic	arcaico
aristocratic	aristocrático
arithmetic	aritmético *(only an adjective)*
aromatic	aromático
artistic	**artístico**
arthritic	artrítico
asthmatic	asmático
astronomic	astronómico
asymmetric	asimétrico
atheistic	ateístico
athletic	**atlético**
Atlantic	Atlántico
atmospheric	atmosférico
atomic	atómico
attic	ático
authentic	**auténtico**
"The food is authentic."	**"La comida es auténtica".**
autistic	autístico
autobiographic	autobiográfico
autocratic	autocrático
automatic	automático
ballistic	balístico

balsamic. . . . . balsámico

Baltic . . . . báltico

barbaric. . . . . barbárico *(more commonly "bárbaro")*

barometric . . . . barométrico

basic . . . . básico

biographic . . . . biográfico

bombastic. . . . . bombástico

botanic. . . . . botánico

bubonic . . . . bubónico

bucolic. . . . . bucólico

bureaucratic . . . . burocrático

calisthenic . . . . calisténico

catastrophic . . . . catastrófico

catatonic . . . . catatónico

cathartic. . . . . catártico

Catholic . . . . **católico**

caustic . . . . cáustico

Celtic. . . . . céltico

ceramic . . . . cerámico *(only an adjective,*
noun is "cerámica")

chaotic. . . . . caótico

characteristic. . . . . característico

charismatic. . . . . carismático

choleric . . . . colérico

chronic. . . . . **crónico**

chronologic . . . . cronológico

citric . . . . cítrico

civic. . . . . cívico

classic . . . . **clásico**

"It's a classic book." . . . . **"Es un libro clásico".**

climatic . . . . climático

colic. . . . . cólico

comic. . . . . cómico *(also used for "comedian")*

concentric. . . . . concéntrico

cosmetic. . . . . cosmético

cosmic . . . . cósmico
critic . . . . crítico *(also used for "critical")*
cryptic . . . . críptico
cubic . . . . cúbico
cylindric . . . . cilíndrico
cynic . . . . cínico

democratic . . . . **democrático**
demographic . . . . demográfico
despotic . . . . despótico
diabetic . . . . diabético
diabolic . . . . diabólico
diagnostic. . . . . diagnóstico
didactic . . . . didáctico
dietetic. . . . . dietético
diplomatic . . . . diplomático
diuretic. . . . . diurético
dogmatic . . . . dogmático
domestic. . . . . **doméstico** *(for politics and flights,*
use "nacional")
doric . . . . dórico
dramatic. . . . . dramático
drastic . . . . **drástico**
   "The situation is not drastic." . . . . **"La situación no es drástica".**
dynamic. . . . . dinámico
dyslexic . . . . disléxico

eccentric. . . . . excéntrico
ecclesiastic . . . . eclesiástico
eclectic. . . . . ecléctico
economic . . . . económico *(also used for "inexpensive")*
ecstatic. . . . . extático
egocentric . . . . egocéntrico
elastic . . . . elástico
electric. . . . . eléctrico
electromagnetic. . . . . electromagnético

electronic . . . . **electrónico**
emblematic . . . . emblemático
emphatic . . . . enfático
energetic . . . . enérgico
enigmatic . . . . enigmático
enthusiastic . . . . entusiástico
epic . . . . épico
epileptic . . . . epiléptico
erotic . . . . erótico
erratic . . . . errático
esoteric . . . . esotérico
ethic . . . . ético
ethnic . . . . étnico
ethnocentric . . . . etnocéntrico
euphoric . . . . eufórico
evangelic . . . . evangélico
exotic . . . . **exótico**

fanatic . . . . fanático
fantastic . . . . **fantástico**
folic . . . . fólico
folkloric . . . . folclórico
forensic . . . . forénsico
frenetic . . . . frenético

galactic . . . . galáctico
gastric . . . . gástrico
gastronomic . . . . gastrónomico
generic . . . . genérico
genetic . . . . genético
geographic . . . . geográfico
geologic . . . . geológico
geometric . . . . geométrico
geriatric . . . . geriátrico
Germanic . . . . germánico
gothic . . . . gótico

Chapter 11

graphic . . . . gráfico
gymnastic. . . . . gimnástico

harmonic . . . . armónico
hedonistic. . . . . hedonístico
hegemonic . . . . hegemónico
hemispheric . . . . hemisférico
heretic . . . . herético
heroic. . . . . **heroico**
    "It was a heroic action." . . . . **"Fue una acción heroica"**.
hieroglyphic . . . . jeroglífico
Hispanic. . . . . hispánico *(more commonly "hispano")*
historic . . . . **histórico**
histrionic. . . . . histriónico
holistic . . . . holístico
homeopathic. . . . . homeopático
Homeric . . . . homérico
hydraulic . . . . hidráulico
hygienic. . . . . higiénico
hyperbolic . . . . hiperbólico
hypnotic. . . . . hipnótico
hypodermic . . . . hipodérmico
hysteric . . . . histérico

ideologic . . . . ideológico
idiomatic . . . . idiomático
idyllic. . . . . idílico
illogic. . . . . ilógico
intrinsic . . . . intrínseco
ionic . . . . iónico
ironic . . . . **irónico**
    "It's an ironic situation." . . . . . **"Es una situación irónica"**.
Islamic . . . . islámico
isometric. . . . . isométrico
italic . . . . itálico

INSTANT Spanish Vocabulary Builder

Jurassic . . . . Jurásico

kinetic . . . . cinético

laconic. . . . . lacónico
lethargic. . . . . letárgico
linguistic. . . . . lingüístico
lithographic . . . . litográfico
logic . . . . lógico *(only an adjective;*
noun is "lógica")
logistic. . . . . logístico
lunatic . . . . lunático
lyric . . . . lírico

macroeconomic. . . . . macroeconómico
magic . . . . mágico *(only an adjective;*
noun is "magia")
magnetic . . . . magnético
mathematic. . . . . matemático
mechanic . . . . mecánico *(also used for "mechanical")*
medic. . . . . médico *(also used for "medical")*
melodic . . . . melódico
melodramatic . . . . melodramático
metabolic . . . . metabólico
metallic . . . . metálico
metalinguistic . . . . metalingüístico
metaphoric . . . . metafórico
metaphysic . . . . metafísico
meteoric. . . . . meteórico
methodic . . . . metódico
metric. . . . . **métrico**
microeconomic . . . . microeconómico
microscopic. . . . . **microscópico**
misanthropic. . . . . misantrópico
mnemonic. . . . . mnémonico
monopolistic . . . . monopolístico

Chapter 11

mosaic . . . . mosaico
multiethnic . . . . multiétnico
mystic . . . . místico
mythic . . . . mítico

napoleonic . . . . napoleónico
narcotic . . . . narcótico
neurologic . . . . neurológico
neurotic . . . . neurótico
Nordic . . . . nórdico
nostalgic . . . . **nostálgico**
numeric . . . . numérico

oceanic . . . . oceánico
olympic . . . . olímpico *(for the sporting event,*
use "olimpiadas")
onomatopoeic . . . . onomatopéyico
optic . . . . óptico
organic . . . . orgánico
orgasmic . . . . orgásmico
orthopedic . . . . ortopédico

Pacific . . . . Pacífico
panic . . . . **pánico**
Paleozoic . . . . Paleozoico
panoramic . . . . panorámico
parasitic . . . . parasítico
pathetic . . . . **patético**
pathologic . . . . patológico
patriotic . . . . **patriótico**
"The people are very patriotic." . . . **"El público es muy patriótico"**.
pediatric . . . . pediátrico
periodic . . . . periódico *(also used*
for "newspaper")
phallic . . . . fálico
philanthropic . . . . filantrópico

INSTANT Spanish Vocabulary Builder

philosophic . . . . filosófico
phobic . . . . fóbico
phonetic . . . . fonético
photogenic . . . . fotogénico
photographic . . . . fotográfico
plastic . . . . plástico
platonic . . . . platónico
pneumatic . . . . pneumático *(also used for "tire")*
poetic . . . . **poético**
polemic . . . . polémico
pornographic . . . . pornográfico
pragmatic . . . . pragmático
prehistoric . . . . prehistórico
problematic . . . . problemático
prolific . . . . prolífico
prophetic . . . . profético
prophylactic . . . . profiláctico
prosaic . . . . prosaico
prosthetic . . . . protésico
psychedelic . . . . psicodélico
psychiatric . . . . psiquiátrico
psychic . . . . psíquico
psychopathic . . . . psicopático
psychotic . . . . psicótico
pubic . . . . púbico
public . . . . público *(also used for "audience")*

rhetoric . . . . retórico
rheumatic . . . . reumático
rhythmic . . . . rítmico
robotic . . . . robótico
romantic . . . . **romántico**
    "It's a romantic city." . . . . **"Es una ciudad romántica".**
rustic . . . . rústico

sadistic . . . . sádico

sarcastic	**sarcástico**
sardonic	sardónico
satanic	satánico
satiric	satírico
scenic	escénico
schematic	esquemático
schizophrenic	esquizofrénico
scholastic	escolástico
scientific	**científico**
semantic	semántico
semiautomatic	semiautomático
semiotic	semiótico
septic	séptico
skeptic	escéptico
sociolinguistic	sociolingüístico
sonic	sónico
soporific	soporífico
spasmodic	espasmódico
spastic	espástico
specific	**específico**
spheric	esférico
sporadic	esporádico
static	estático
statistic	estadístico
stoic	estoico
strategic	**estratégico**
stylistic	estilístico
subatomic	subatómico
supersonic	supersónico
symbolic	**simbólico**
"It's a symbolic gift."	**"Es un regalo simbólico".**
symmetric	simétrico
symptomatic	sintomático
synthetic	sintético
systematic	sistemático

telegenic . . . . telegénico
telegraphic . . . . telegráfico
telepathic . . . . telepático
telescopic . . . . telescópico
terrific . . . . terrífico *(meaning "terrifying")*
thematic . . . . temático
theoretic . . . . teórico
therapeutic . . . . terapéutico
titanic . . . . titánico
tonic . . . . tónico
topic . . . . tópico
touristic . . . . turístico
toxic . . . . tóxico
traffic . . . . tráfico
tragic . . . . trágico
traumatic . . . . traumático
tropic . . . . trópico

ultrasonic . . . . ultrasónico

volcanic . . . . volcánico

11A.

Una las palabras que están relacionadas o que son sinónimos.

1. pragmático	práctico
2. tráfico	detalles
3. auténtico	amoroso
4. específico	carros
5. electrónico	intemporal
6. clásico	estéreo
7. romántico	verdadero

11B.

Escuche y lea el cuento. Responda las siguientes preguntas, usando oraciones completas.

Después de dos días en Ibiza, Juan y Angélica van a Alicante. Alicante es bellísima, de una belleza <u>clásica</u>. Durante el día (during the day) **van a algunos museos <u>artísticos</u>, y por la noche ven lo <u>mágico</u> que es Alicante. No hay una explicación <u>específica</u>, pero Alicante es una ciudad <u>fantástica</u>. Juan conduce un carro alquilado** (rented car)**, pero hay mucho <u>tráfico</u>. Angélica dice que no es un plan muy <u>estratégico</u>. En Alicante hay siempre mucho <u>tráfico</u> en el verano. Ella dice, "El tren es mejor** (better)**, no es muy <u>romántico</u> pasar las vacaciones dentro de un carro". Juan responde, "Veremos…".**

1. ¿Cuál es el problema cuando Juan conduce?

2. ¿Por qué dice Angélica, "El tren es mejor"?

3. ¿Qué tipos de museos visitan?

4. ¿Cuándo es mágico Alicante?

5. ¿Qué tipo de ciudad es Alicante?

Chapter 12 — -ical/-ico

Many English words ending in "–ical" correspond to "–ico" in Spanish.

Spanish words ending in "–ico" are usually adjectives. For example,

identical twins = *gemelos idénticos*

ENGLISH . . . . SPANISH

All words and phrases in bold are on **Track 12** *of the accompanying CD.*

acoustical . . . . acústico
aeronautical . . . . aeronáutico
allegorical . . . . alegórico
alphabetical . . . . **alfabético**
    "It's in alphabetical order." . . . **"Está en orden alfabético"**.
analytical . . . . analítico
anarchical . . . . anárquico
anatomical . . . . anatómico
antithetical . . . . antitético
apolitical . . . . apolítico
archaeological . . . . **arqueológico**
astrological . . . . astrológico
astronomical . . . . astronómico
asymmetrical . . . . asimétrico
atypical . . . . atípico
autobiographical . . . . autobiográfico

biblical . . . . bíblico
bibliographical . . . . bibliográfico
biochemical . . . . bioquímico
biographical . . . . biográfico
biological . . . . **biológico**

botanical . . . . **botánico**

categorical . . . . categórico
chemical. . . . . químico
chronological . . . . cronológico
classical . . . . clásico
clinical . . . . clínico
comical . . . . cómico *(also used for "comedian")*
critical . . . . **crítico** *(also used for "critic")*
cubical. . . . . cúbico
cyclical. . . . . cíclico
cylindrical. . . . . cilíndrico
cynical . . . . **cínico**

demographical . . . . demográfico
diabolical. . . . . diabólico
dialectical. . . . . dialéctico

ecclesiastical. . . . . eclesiástico
ecological. . . . . ecológico
economical . . . . económico
electrical. . . . . **eléctrico**
elliptical . . . . elíptico
empirical . . . . empírico
ethical . . . . ético
evangelical. . . . . evangélico

fanatical. . . . . fanático

gastronomical . . . . gastronómico
genealogical. . . . . genealógico
geographical . . . . geográfico
geological . . . . geológico
geometrical. . . . . geométrico
grammatical . . . . gramático

hierarchical	jerárquico
historical	histórico
hypothetical	hipotético
hysterical	histérico

identical	**idéntico**

"They are identical twins." . . . **"Son gemelos idénticos".**

ideological	ideológico
illogical	ilógico
impractical	impráctico
ironical	irónico
lexical	léxico (meaning "lexicon," "vocabulary")
logical	**lógico**
logistical	logístico
lyrical	lírico

magical	**mágico**
mathematical	matemático
mechanical	mecánico (also used for "mechanic")
medical	médico (also used for "doctor," "medic")
metaphorical	metafórico
metaphysical	metafísico
methodical	metódico
musical	músico
mystical	místico
mythical	mítico
mythological	mitológico

nautical	náutico
neurological	neurológico
numerical	numérico

optical	óptico

paradoxical	paradójico
pathological	patológico
pedagogical	pedagógico
periodical	periódico *(also used for "newspaper")*
pharmaceutical	farmacéutico *(also used for "pharmacist")*
philosophical	filosófico
physical	físico
physiological	fisiológico
poetical	poético
political	político
practical	**práctico**

"She is very practical." . . . . . **"Ella es muy práctica".**

prehistorical	prehistórico
psychological	psicológico
reciprocal	recíproco
rhetorical	retórico
rhythmical	rítmico
sabbatical	sabático
satirical	satírico
skeptical	escéptico
sociological	sociológico
sociopolitical	sociopolítico
spherical	esférico
statistical	estadístico
stereotypical	estereotípico
stoical	estoico
strategical	estratégico
symmetrical	simétrico
tactical	táctico
technical	**técnico** *(also used for "technician")*
technological	tecnológico
theological	teológico

theoretical . . . . teórico

topical . . . . tópico

typical . . . . **típico**

    "What a typical response!" . . . **"¡Qué respuesta típica!"**

typographical . . . . tipográfico

tyrannical . . . . tiránico

12A.

Una las palabras que están relacionadas o que son sinónimos.

1. típico	pragmático
2. idéntico	importante
3. práctico	usual
4. biográfico	personal
5. diabólico	médico
6. clínico	demoníaco
7. crítico	igual

12B.

Escuche y lea el cuento. Responda las siguientes preguntas, usando oraciones completas.

Juan dice, "Alicante es tan bonita que podemos pasar el mes entero (the whole month) **aquí**". Angélica comprende pero dice, "No, quiero ser <u>práctica</u>, debemos continuar nuestro viaje de una manera <u>lógica</u>". Juan ve que ella es muy <u>lógica</u> ahora y dice, "Angélica, ésto es <u>típico</u> de tí, ¡eres siempre tan <u>práctica</u>!" Ella responde, "¡No seas tan <u>crítico</u>! Tú también quieres ir a la Costa del Sol, ¿verdad?" Juan responde, "**Tienes razón** (you're right), **vamos a la Costa del Sol**".

1. ¿ Juan quiere permanecer (to stay) en Alicante o partir?

2. ¿De qué manera quiere viajar Angélica?

3. ¿Angélica es siempre práctica?

4. ¿Adónde van ahora?

5. ¿Qué dice Angélica de la Costa del Sol?

-id/-ido

Many English words ending in "–id" correspond to "–ido" in Spanish.

Spanish words ending in "–ido" are usually adjectives. For example,

a splendid plan = *un plan espléndido*

ENGLISH . . . . SPANISH

*All words and phrases in bold are on **Track 13** of the accompanying CD.*

acid . . . . ácido
antacid . . . . antiácido
arid . . . . árido
avid . . . . ávido

candid . . . . cándido *(meaning "innocent," "naïve")*

Cupid . . . . Cupido

fervid . . . . férvido
flaccid . . . . flácido
florid . . . . florido
fluid . . . . fluido
frigid . . . . frígido

hybrid . . . . híbrido

insipid . . . . insípido
intrepid . . . . intrépido
invalid . . . . inválido

languid . . . . lánguido

liquid . . . . **líquido**
livid . . . . lívido
lucid . . . . lúcido

morbid . . . . mórbido

pallid . . . . pálido
placid . . . . plácido
putrid . . . . pútrido

rapid . . . . **rápido**
rigid . . . . **rígido**

solid . . . . sólido
sordid . . . . sórdido
splendid . . . . **espléndido**
    "He has a splendid plan." . . . **"Él tiene un plan espléndido"**.
squallid . . . . escuálido
stupid . . . . **estúpido**

timid . . . . **tímido**
    "Mateo is very timid." . . . . . . **"Mateo es muy tímido"**.
torrid . . . . tórrido

valid . . . . **válido**
vivid . . . . vívido

13A.

Una las palabras que están relacionadas o que son sinónimos.

1. rápido	maravilloso
2. tímido	limón
3. estúpido	veloz
4. ácido	introvertido
5. frígido	seco
6. árido	helado
7. espléndido	idiota

13B.

Escuche y lea el cuento. Responda las siguientes preguntas, usando oraciones completas.

Para ir a la Costa del Sol, Juan y Angélica deciden alquilar (to rent) **otro carro. Angélica dice que es un plan <u>estúpido</u>, pero Juan piensa que es un plan <u>espléndido</u>. Angélica dice, "Pero yo quiero viajar más <u>rápido</u>…". Juan dice que prefiere conducir cuando hace calor. Durante el viaje hace un tiempo** (the weather is) **muy <u>húmedo</u>; de repente Juan se pone muy <u>pálido</u> y le duele el estómago. Angélica no dice nada y va a una farmacia y compra un poco de <u>antiácido</u> para Juan. El farmacéutico dice que él debe beber mucho <u>líquido</u> y no comer comida <u>ácida</u>.**

1. ¿Qué dice Angélica del plan de ir a la Costa del Sol en carro?

2. ¿Qué piensa Juan de su idea?

3. ¿Qué tiempo hace durante el viaje?

4. ¿Qué le compra Angélica a Juan cuando él se siente mal?

5. ¿El farmacéutico dice que debe beber qué? ¿Y qué no debe comer?

Chapter 14

English words ending in "–ism" often correspond to "–ismo" in Spanish.

Spanish words ending in "–ismo" are usually masculine nouns. For example,

optimism = *el optimismo*

ENGLISH . . . . SPANISH	

*All words and phrases in bold are on **Track 14** of the accompanying CD.*

absenteeism . . . . absentismo
absolutism . . . . absolutismo
activism . . . . activismo
adventurism . . . . aventurismo
alcoholism . . . . **alcoholismo**
altruism . . . . altruismo
Americanism. . . . . americanismo
amorphism . . . . amorfismo
anachronism. . . . . anacronismo
anarchism. . . . . anarquismo
Anglicism . . . . anglicismo
antagonism. . . . . antagonismo
anticapitalism . . . . anticapitalismo
anticommunism . . . . anticomunismo
antifascism . . . . **antifascismo**
   "There was a lot of antifascism.". . . **"Había mucho antifascismo"**.
anti-Semitism. . . . . antisemitismo
antiterrorism . . . . antiterrorismo
astigmatism. . . . . astigmatismo
atheism . . . . ateísmo
athleticism . . . . **atletismo** *(also used for "track-and-field")*
autism . . . . autismo

baptism	bautismo
bipolarism	bipolarismo
botulism	botulismo
Buddhism	budismo
cannibalism	canibalismo
capitalism	**capitalismo**
"Capitalism comes from America."	**"El capitalismo viene de América".**
Catholicism	catolicismo
catechism	catecismo
centralism	centralismo
chauvinism	chovinismo
classicism	clasicismo
colonialism	colonialismo
communism	**comunismo**
conformism	conformismo
conservatism	conservatismo
criticism	criticismo *(more commonly "crítica")*
cubism	cubismo
cynicism	cinismo
Darwinism	darwinismo
deism	deísmo
despotism	despotismo
determinism	determinismo
dogmatism	dogmatismo
dualism	dualismo
egoism	egoísmo *(meaning "selfishness")*
egotism	egotismo
elitism	elitismo
eroticism	erotismo
euphemism	eufemismo
evangelism	evangelismo
evolutionism	evolucionismo

INSTANT Spanish Vocabulary Builder

exorcism. . . . . exorcismo
expressionism . . . . expresionismo
extremism. . . . . extremismo

fanaticism. . . . . fanatismo
fascism. . . . . **fascismo**
   "I don't like fascism.". . . . . . . **"No me gusta el fascismo"**.
fatalism . . . . fatalismo
favoritism . . . . favoritismo
federalism. . . . . federalismo
feminism . . . . **feminismo**
feudalism . . . . feudalismo
fundamentalism. . . . . fundamentalismo
futurism . . . . futurismo

globalism . . . . globalismo

hedonism . . . . hedonismo
heroism . . . . heroísmo
Hinduism . . . . hinduismo
humanism. . . . . humanismo
humanitarianism . . . . humanitarismo
hypnotism. . . . . hipnotismo

idealism . . . . idealismo
imperialism. . . . . imperialismo
impressionism . . . . **impresionismo**
individualism. . . . . individualismo
Italianism . . . . italianismo

Judaism . . . . judaismo

Latinism . . . . latinismo
lesbianism . . . . lesbianismo
liberalism . . . . liberalismo
localism . . . . localismo

magnetism . . . . magnetismo
Marxism . . . . marxismo
materialism . . . . materialismo
mechanism . . . . **mecanismo**
metabolism . . . . metabolismo
microorganism . . . . microorganismo
minimalism . . . . minimalismo
modernism . . . . modernismo
monotheism . . . . monoteísmo
multiculturalism . . . . multiculturalismo

nationalism . . . . **nacionalismo**
    "There is a lot of nationalism." . . . **"Hay mucho nacionalismo"**.
naturalism . . . . naturalismo
Nazism . . . . nazismo
negativism . . . . negativismo
neofascism . . . . neofascismo
neologism . . . . neologismo
neo-Nazism . . . . neonazismo
neorealism . . . . neorrealismo
nepotism . . . . nepotismo
nudism . . . . nudismo

objectivism . . . . objetivismo
occultism . . . . ocultismo
opportunism . . . . oportunismo
optimism . . . . **optimismo**
    "Optimism always helps." . . . **"El optimismo ayuda siempre"**.
organism . . . . **organismo**

paganism . . . . paganismo
parallelism . . . . paralelismo
passivism . . . . pasivismo
patriotism . . . . patriotismo
pessimism . . . . pesimismo
pluralism . . . . pluralismo

INSTANT Spanish Vocabulary Builder

polytheism	politeísmo
populism	populismo
positivism	positivismo
postmodernism	posmodernismo
pragmatism	pragmatismo
primitivism	primitivismo
professionalism	**profesionalismo**
protectionism	proteccionismo
Protestantism	protestantismo
provincialism	provincialismo
purism	purismo
Puritanism	puritanismo

racism	**racismo**
radicalism	radicalismo
rationalism	racionalismo
realism	realismo
reformism	reformismo
regionalism	regionalismo
relativism	relativismo
romanticism	romanticismo

sadism	sadismo
satanism	satanismo
sensationalism	sensacionalismo
sensualism	sensualismo
separatism	separatismo
sexism	sexismo
socialism	**socialismo**
spiritualism	espiritualismo
Stalinism	estalinismo
stoicism	estoicismo
structuralism	estructuralismo
surrealism	surrealismo
syllogism	silogismo
symbolism	simbolismo

synchronism . . . . sincronismo

terrorism . . . . **terrorismo**
    "Terrorism is senseless." . . . . . **"El terrorismo no tiene sentido".**
totalitarianism . . . . totalitarismo
tourism. . . . . **turismo**
traditionalism . . . . tradicionalismo
transcendentalism . . . . trascendentalismo
traumatism . . . . traumatismo
truism. . . . . truismo

utilitarianism . . . . utilitarismo

vandalism. . . . . vandalismo
vegetarianism . . . . vegetarianismo
voyeurism. . . . . voyeurismo

14A.

Una las palabras que están relacionadas o que son sinónimos.

1. turismo   olímpico
2. comunismo   nación
3. patriotismo   Karl Marx
4. atletismo   comentario
5. terrorismo   positivo
6. optimismo   bomba
7. criticismo   vacaciones

14B.

Escuche y lea el cuento. Responda las siguientes preguntas, usando oraciones completas.

Después de su primer día en la Costa del Sol, Juan se siente mejor. Hay mucho <u>turismo</u> en la Costa del Sol, y mucha historia, pero ellos deciden relajarse (decide to relax) **por algunos días en la playa. Angélica compra un libro de historia española y lee sobre el comienzo** (about the beginning) **del <u>fascismo</u> en España durante los años treinta. También lee sobre la influencia del <u>comunismo</u> y del <u>socialismo</u> en España. Ellos hablan sobre el <u>patriotismo</u> español, y Angélica le pregunta a Juan qué piensa sobre** (what he thinks about) **el <u>capitalismo</u>. Juan dice, "Angélica, todo esto es muy interesante pero... ¡tomemos un helado!"**

1. ¿Hay mucho turismo en la Costa del Sol?

2. ¿Cuándo comenzó el fascismo en España?

3. ¿ Angélica lee sobre la influencia de qué en España?

4. ¿Sobre qué hablan?

5. ¿Qué dice Juan al final?

-ist/-ista

Many English words ending in "–ist" correspond to "–ista" in Spanish.

Spanish words ending in "–ista" are usually nouns. For example,

an artist = *un/una artista*

ENGLISH . . . . SPANISH

All words and phrases in bold are on **Track 15** *of the accompanying CD.*

abolitionist . . . . abolicionista
activist . . . . activista
acupuncturist. . . . . acupuncturista
adventurist . . . . aventurista
alchemist . . . . alquemista
altruist . . . . altruista
analyst . . . . analista
anarchist . . . . anarquista
anatomist . . . . anatomista
antagonist . . . . antagonista
anticommunist . . . . anticomunista
antifascist . . . . antifascista
artist . . . . **artista**
   "That artist is creative." . . . . . **"Ese artista es creativo".**
atheist . . . . ateísta *(more commonly "ateo")*

Baptist . . . . bautista
botanist . . . . botanista
Buddhist. . . . . budista

capitalist. . . . . **capitalista**
caricaturist . . . . caricaturista

cellist . . . . violoncelista

centralist . . . . centralista

chauvinist . . . . chovinista

columnist . . . . columnista

communist . . . . **comunista**

conformist . . . . conformista

conservationist . . . . conservacionista

contortionist . . . . contorsionista

cubist . . . . cubista

cyclist . . . . ciclista

dentist . . . . **dentista**

    "Her son is a dentist." . . . . . . **"Su hijo es un dentista".**

dualist . . . . dualista

duelist . . . . duelista

ecologist . . . . ecologista

economist . . . . economista

egoist . . . . egoísta

egotist . . . . egotista

elitist . . . . elitista

essayist . . . . ensayista

evangelist . . . . evangelista

exhibitionist . . . . exhibicionista

existentialist . . . . existencialista

expansionist . . . . expansionista

expressionist . . . . expresionista

extremist . . . . extremista

fascist . . . . fascista

fatalist . . . . fatalista

federalist . . . . federalista

feminist . . . . feminista

finalist . . . . **finalista**

flutist . . . . flautista

florist . . . . **florista**

formalist. . . . . formalista

fundamentalist. . . . . fundamentalista

futurist . . . . futurista

geneticist . . . . geneticista

guitarist . . . . **guitarrista**

"Carlos Santana is   **"Carlos Santana es**
a great guitarist." . . . . **un gran guitarrista".**

harpist . . . . arpista

hedonist . . . . hedonista

humanist. . . . . humanista

humorist . . . . humorista

hygienist. . . . . higienista

idealist . . . . **idealista**

illusionist . . . . ilusionista

imperialist. . . . . imperialista

impressionist. . . . . impresionista

individualist . . . . individualista

internist . . . . internista

isolationist . . . . aislacionista

jurist. . . . . jurista

Latinist . . . . latinista

Leninist. . . . . leninista

linguist. . . . . lingüista

list . . . . **lista**

"She has a list of questions." . . . **"Ella tiene una lista de preguntas".**

machinist . . . . maquinista

manicurist. . . . . manicurista

Marxist. . . . . marxista

masochist . . . . masoquista

materialist. . . . . materialista

Methodist	metodista
minimalist	**minimalista**
modernist	modernista
monopolist	monopolista
moralist	moralista
motorist	motorista
muralist	muralista
narcissist	narcisista
nationalist	nacionalista
naturalist	naturalista
novelist	novelista
nudist	nudista
nutritionist	**nutricionista**
opportunist	oportunista
optimist	**optimista**
organist	organista
orthodontist	ortodontista
pacifist	pacifista
perfectionist	perfeccionista
pessimist	**pesimista**
pianist	**pianista**

"He wants to be a pianist." . . **"Quisiera ser pianista"**.

pluralist	pluralista
populist	populista
positivist	positivista
pragmatist	pragmatista
prohibitionist	prohibicionista
protagonist	protagonista
protectionist	proteccionista
publicist	publicista
purist	purista
racist	**racista**

INSTANT Spanish Vocabulary Builder

rationalist . . . . racionalista
realist. . . . . **realista**
receptionist. . . . . recepcionista
reformist. . . . . reformista
reservist . . . . reservista

sadomasochist. . . . . sadomasoquista
satanist. . . . . satanista
satirist . . . . satirista
secessionist. . . . . secesionista
semifinalist . . . . semifinalista
separatist . . . . separatista
sexist . . . . sexista
socialist . . . . socialista
soloist . . . . solista
specialist . . . . especialista
Stalinist . . . . estalinista
stylist . . . . estilista
surrealist. . . . . surrealista
symbolist . . . . simbolista

terrorist . . . . **terrorista**
tourist . . . . **turista**
    "In Spain, I'm a tourist." . . . . **"En España, soy turista"**.
traditionalist . . . . tradicionalista

violinist. . . . . violinista
vocalist. . . . . vocalista

15A.

Una las palabras que están relacionadas o que son sinónimos.

1. artista	dinero
2. dentista	pasaporte
3. turista	campeón
4. pesimista	cantante
5. idealista	positivo
6. finalista	diente
7. capitalista	negativo

15B.

Escuche y lea el cuento. Responda las siguientes preguntas, usando oraciones completas.

Destinación: ¡Andalucía! Mientras Juan y Angélica pasean por (walk around) **Andalucía conocen otra pareja** (another couple) **de Bilbao. El muchacho es <u>dentista</u> y la muchacha es <u>artista</u>; los nuevos amigos de Juan y Angélica son <u>turistas</u> "profesionales"; viajan mucho y saben mucho sobre Andalucía. Angélica tiene una <u>lista</u> de preguntas y el <u>dentista</u> puede dar una respuesta a cada** (every) **pregunta. Son muy inteligentes pero son una pareja extraña. La muchacha es <u>optimista</u> mientras que el muchacho es <u>pesimista</u>. Ella es <u>idealista</u> y él es <u>realista</u>. El <u>dentista</u> les dice a Juan y Angélica, "¿Queréis ir a Málaga con nosostros?" Juan responde, "Veremos...".**

1. ¿Qué hace el muchacho que conocen?

2. ¿Los nuevos amigos de Juan y Angélica viajan a menudo (often)?

3. ¿De qué tiene una lista Angélica?

4. ¿Cómo es el dentista?

5. ¿Cómo es la artista?

-ive/-ivo

English words ending in "–ive" often correspond to "–ivo" in Spanish.

Spanish words ending in "–ivo" are usually adjectives. For example,

a <u>competitive</u> boy = *un niño <u>competitivo</u>*

ENGLISH . . . . SPANISH	

All words and phrases in bold are on **Track 16** *of the accompanying CD.*

abortive . . . . abortivo
abrasive. . . . . abrasivo
abusive . . . . abusivo
accumulative. . . . . acumulativo
accusative . . . . acusativo
active. . . . . **activo**
    "It's not an active volcano." . . . **"No es un volcán activo"**.
addictive . . . . adictivo
additive . . . . aditivo
adhesive. . . . . adhesivo
adjective. . . . . **adjetivo**
administrative . . . . administrativo
adoptive. . . . . adoptivo
affective . . . . afectivo
affirmative . . . . afirmativo
aggressive . . . . **agresivo**
allusive. . . . . alusivo
alternative . . . . alternativo
anticorrosive . . . . anticorrosivo
appositive. . . . . apositivo
apprehensive . . . . aprensivo
archive. . . . . archivo

assertive	asertivo
associative	asociativo
attractive	atractivo
attributive	atributivo
augmentative	aumentativo
authoritive	autoritativo *(more commonly "autoritario")*

captive	cautivo
causative	causativo
coactive	coactivo
cognitive	cognitivo
cohesive	cohesivo
collaborative	colaborativo
collective	colectivo
combative	combativo
commemorative	conmemorativo
communicative	comunicativo
comparative	comparativo
competitive	**competitivo**
"The kids are so competitive."	**"Los niños son tan competitivos".**
comprehensive	comprensivo *(meaning "understanding")*
compulsive	compulsivo
conclusive	conclusivo
conductive	conductivo
conflictive	conflictivo
connective	conectivo
consecutive	**consecutivo**
conservative	conservativo *(more commonly "conservador")*
constructive	constructivo
contemplative	contemplativo
contributive	contributivo
convulsive	convulsivo
cooperative	**cooperativo**

INSTANT Spanish Vocabulary Builder

coordinative . . . . coordinativo
corrective . . . . correctivo
corrosive . . . . corrosivo
corruptive . . . . corruptivo
creative . . . . **creativo**
cumulative . . . . acumulativo
curative . . . . curativo
cursive . . . . cursivo

dative . . . . dativo
decisive . . . . decisivo
declarative . . . . declarativo
decorative . . . . decorativo
deductive . . . . deductivo
defensive . . . . defensivo *(only used to describe things)*
definitive . . . . **definitivo**
   "It's a definitive plan." . . . . . . **"Es un plan definitivo".**
degenerative. . . . . degenerativo
deliberative. . . . . deliberativo
demonstrative . . . . demostrativo
denominative . . . . denominativo
depressive . . . . depresivo
derivative . . . . derivativo
descriptive . . . . descriptivo
destructive . . . . destructivo
determinative . . . . determinativo
diffusive . . . . difusivo
digestive. . . . . digestivo
diminutive. . . . . diminutivo
directive . . . . directivo
distinctive . . . . distintivo
distributive . . . . distributivo
divisive. . . . . divisivo

educative . . . . educativo

effective . . . . efectivo *(also used for "cash")*

elective. . . . . electivo

elusive . . . . elusivo

emotive . . . . emotivo *(meaning "emotional")*

erosive. . . . . erosivo

evasive. . . . . evasivo

evocative . . . . evocativo

excessive . . . . **excesivo**

exclusive . . . . exclusivo

executive . . . . **ejecutivo**

exhaustive . . . . exhaustivo

expansive. . . . . expansivo

explicative . . . . explicativo

explorative . . . . explorativo *(more commonly
"exploratorio")*

explosive . . . . explosivo

expressive . . . . expresivo

extensive . . . . extensivo

festive . . . . festivo *(also used for "of a holiday")*

figurative . . . . figurativo

formative . . . . formativo

fugitive. . . . . fugitivo

furtive. . . . . furtivo

generative . . . . generativo

hyperactive. . . . . hiperactivo

illuminative . . . . iluminativo

illustrative . . . . ilustrativo

imaginative. . . . . **imaginativo**

   "What an imaginative plan!" . . . **"¡Qué plan tan imaginativo!"**

imitative . . . . imitativo

imperative . . . . imperativo

implosive . . . . implosivo

INSTANT Spanish Vocabulary Builder

impulsive . . . . impulsivo
inactive . . . . inactivo
incentive. . . . . incentivo
incisive. . . . . incisivo
inclusive . . . . inclusivo
indicative . . . . indicativo
infinitive . . . . infinitivo
informative . . . . informativo
inoffensive . . . . inofensivo
inquisitive . . . . inquisitivo
instinctive . . . . instintivo
instructive . . . . instructivo
intensive . . . . intensivo
interactive. . . . . **interactivo**
interpretative . . . . interpretativo
interrogative . . . . interrogativo
intransitive . . . . intransitivo
introspective . . . . introspectivo
intuitive . . . . intuitivo
inventive . . . . inventivo

legislative . . . . legislativo
lucrative . . . . lucrativo

massive . . . . masivo
motive . . . . motivo
multiplicative . . . . multiplicativo

narrative . . . . narrativo
native . . . . nativo
negative . . . . **negativo**
 "Don't be so negative!" . . . . . **"¡No seas tan negativo!"**
nominative . . . . nominativo

objective. . . . . **objetivo**
obsessive . . . . obsesivo

offensive . . . . **ofensivo**
olive . . . . olivo *(meaning "olive tree")*
operative . . . . operativo
oppressive . . . . opresivo

partitive . . . . partitivo
passive. . . . . pasivo
pejorative. . . . . peyorativo
pensive . . . . pensativo
perceptive . . . . perceptivo
permissive . . . . permisivo
persuasive . . . . persuasivo
positive . . . . **positivo**
possessive . . . . **posesivo**
preparative. . . . . preparativo
prescriptive. . . . . preceptivo
presumptive . . . . presuntivo
preventive. . . . . preventivo
primitive. . . . . **primitivo**
productive . . . . **productivo**
progressive. . . . . progresivo
prohibitive . . . . prohibitivo
prospective. . . . . prospectivo
provocative. . . . . provocativo
punitive . . . . punitivo

qualitative. . . . . cualitativo
quantitative. . . . . cuantitativo

radioactive . . . . radiactivo
reactive . . . . reactivo
receptive . . . . receptivo
recessive . . . . recesivo
recreative . . . . recreativo
reflexive . . . . reflexivo
regressive. . . . . regresivo

relative . . . . relativo *(only an adjective)*

repetitive . . . . **repetitivo**

    "It's a repetitive exercise." . . . **"Es un ejercicio repetitivo".**

repulsive. . . . . repulsivo

representative . . . . representativo *(only an adjective)*

repressive. . . . . represivo

reproductive . . . . reproductivo

respective. . . . . respectivo

restorative. . . . . restaurativo

restrictive . . . . restrictivo

retentive . . . . retentivo

retroactive . . . . retroactivo

retrospective . . . . retrospectivo

sedative . . . . sedativo

seductive . . . . seductivo *(more commonly*
                                       "seductor(a)")

selective . . . . **selectivo**

sensitive . . . . sensitivo *(meaning "perceptive")*

speculative . . . . especulativo

subjective . . . . **subjetivo**

subjunctive . . . . subjuntivo

subversive. . . . . subversivo

successive. . . . . sucesivo

suggestive. . . . . sugestivo *(also used for "attractive")*

superlative . . . . superlativo

tentative . . . . tentativo

transitive. . . . . transitivo

unproductive. . . . . improductivo

vegetative. . . . . vegetativo

votive. . . . . votivo

16A.

Una las palabras que están relacionadas o que son sinónimos.

1. creativo	pesimista
2. consecutivo	optimista
3. negativo	imaginativo
4. positivo	siguiente
5. competitivo	causa
6. productivo	ganador
7. motivo	eficiente

16B.

Escuche y lea el cuento. Responda las siguientes preguntas, usando oraciones completas.

Juan encuentra a Andalucía absolutamente fascinante. Había escuchado (he had heard) **muchas cosas <u>negativas</u> sobre Andalucía, pero él ve una región <u>creativa</u> y <u>productiva</u>. También Angélica tiene una impresión <u>positiva</u> de Andalucía. Antes de partir Juan quiere ir a buscar el pueblo** (the village) **donde nació su abuelo. "Un buen <u>motivo</u> para ir",** dice Angélica. **Van a Jerez, un pueblo poco <u>activo</u> pero muy acogedor** (welcoming). **Pasan dos días <u>consecutivos</u> allí.**

1. ¿Qué había escuchado Juan sobre Andalucía?

2. ¿Qué piensa Juan ahora sobre Andalucía?

3. ¿Qué impresión tiene Angélica de Andalucía?

4. ¿Cómo es el pueblo de Jerez?

5. ¿Cuántos días pasan allí?

-ment/-mento

English words ending in "–ment" often correspond to "–mento" in Spanish.

Spanish words ending in "–mento" are usually masculine nouns. For example,

a monument = *un monumento*

ENGLISH . . . . SPANISH

All words and phrases in bold are on **Track 17** *of the accompanying CD.*

apartment . . . . **apartamento**
   "What a beautiful apartment." . . . **"¡Qué apartamento tan bonito!"**
argument . . . . argumento *(also used for "plot/story line")*
armament . . . . armamento

cement . . . . **cemento**
compartment . . . . compartimento
complement . . . . complemento
condiment . . . . condimento

department . . . . **departamento** *(also used for "apartment")*
   "I'm looking for   **"Busco el Departamento**
   the Spanish Department." . . . . **de Español".**
detriment . . . . detrimento
document . . . . **documento**

element . . . . **elemento**
excrement . . . . excremento
experiment . . . . experimento

ferment	fermento *(only a noun)*
filament	filamento
firmament	firmamento
fragment	**fragmento**
impediment	impedimento
implement	implemento
increment	incremento
instrument	**instrumento**
lament	lamento
ligament	ligamento
microelement	microelemento
moment	**momento**
"One moment, please."	**"Un momento, por favor".**
monument	**monumento**
ornament	**ornamento**
parliament	parlamento
pavement	pavimento
pigment	pigmento
rudiment	rudimento
sacrament	sacramento
sediment	sedimento
segment	**segmento**
supplement	suplemento
temperament	temperamento
testament	testamento
torment	tormento

Sometimes English words ending in "–ment" will correspond to "–miento" in Spanish. Following are seventeen (17) of the most commonly used words that follow this pattern:

commandment > mandamiento
comportment > comportamiento
discernment > discernimiento
enchantment > encantamiento
enrichment > enriquecimiento
entertainment > entretenimiento
equipment > equipamiento
establishment > establecimiento
movement > movimiento
presentiment > presentimiento
recruitment > reclutamiento
refinement > refinamiento
regiment > regimiento
requirement > requerimiento
resentment > resentimiento
sentiment > sentimiento
treatment > tratamiento

17A.

Una las palabras que están relacionadas o que son sinónimos.

1. instrumento	medicina
2. apartamento	papel
3. momento	renta
4. documento	instante
5. tratamiento	guitarra
6. segmento	héroes
7. monumento	parte

17B.

Escuche y lea el cuento. Responda las siguientes preguntas, usando oraciones completas.

En camino hacia el norte (on the way north) **el <u>argumento</u> era si ir a Córdoba o no. El tío de Angélica vive allá y tiene un <u>apartamento</u> para ellos. Él es profesor en el <u>departamento</u> de finanzas en la universidad en Córdoba. El problema es que él siempre tiene algún comentario sobre el comportamiento de ellos. Él es muy formal, y nunca da un halago** (compliment)**. Juan no quiere ir porque piensa que será un <u>tormento</u>. Angélica dice, "Vamos, Juan, hazme este favor** (do me this favor)**, y después vamos adonde tú quieras". Por un <u>momento</u> Juan quiere decir que no, pero al final dice, "Está bien, cariño, vamos a Córdoba".**

1. ¿Cuál es el argumento en camino hacia el norte?

2. ¿Dónde vive el tío de Angélica?

3. ¿Qué hace su tío?

4. ¿Por qué Juan no quiere ir a Córdoba?

5. Al final, ¿deciden ir a Córdoba o no?

Chapter 18

Many English words ending in "–or" have the same ending in Spanish.

Spanish words ending in "–or" are usually masculine nouns. For example,

a motor = *un motor*

ENGLISH . . . . SPANISH

*All words and phrases in bold are on **Track 18** of the accompanying CD.*

accelerator . . . . acelerador
accumulator . . . . acumulador *(also used for "car battery")*
actor . . . . **actor**
    "He's a good actor." . . . . **"Es buen actor".**
adaptor . . . . adaptador
administrator. . . . . administrador
aggressor . . . . agresor
agitator . . . . agitador
alternator . . . . alternador
ambassador . . . . embajador
animator. . . . . animador *(also used for "presenter")*
anterior . . . . anterior
applicator. . . . . aplicador
ardor . . . . ardor
aspirator . . . . aspirador *(also used for "vacuum cleaner")*
assessor . . . . asesor *(meaning "consultant")*
auditor. . . . . auditor
author . . . . **autor**
aviator. . . . . aviador

benefactor . . . . benefactor

calculator . . . . calculador

calibrator . . . . calibrador

candor . . . . candor *(meaning "innocence")*

cantor . . . . cantor

captivator . . . . cautivador

carburator . . . . carburador

censor . . . . censor

clamor . . . . clamor

co-editor . . . . coeditor

collaborator . . . . colaborador

collector . . . . coleccionador

color . . . . **color**

    "What a nice color." . . . . **"Qué color tan bonito".**

commentator . . . . comentador

communicator . . . . comunicador

competitor . . . . competidor

condor . . . . cóndor

conductor . . . . conductor *(for music, use "director")*

confessor . . . . confesor

connector . . . . conectador

conquistador . . . . conquistador

constructor . . . . constructor

contaminator . . . . contaminador

contributor . . . . contribuidor

cooperator . . . . cooperador

coordinator . . . . coordinador

corrector . . . . corrector

corruptor . . . . corruptor

creator . . . . **creador**

cultivator . . . . cultivador

cursor . . . . cursor

debtor . . . . deudor

decorator . . . . decorador

denominator . . . . denominador

detonator	detonador
detractor	detractor
devastator	devastador
dictator	**dictador**
director	**director**
dishonor	deshonor
distributor	distribuidor
divisor	divisor
doctor	**doctor**
dolor	dolor *(meaning "pain")*
donor	donador
editor	editor
educator	educador
elector	elector
elevator	elevador
emperor	emperador
equator	ecuador
error	**error**
"It's a big error."	**"Es un gran error".**
excavator	excavador
exterior	**exterior**
exterminator	exterminador
extractor	extractor
facilitator	facilitador
factor	factor
favor	**favor**
fervor	fervor
fumigator	fumigador
furor	furor
generator	generador
gladiator	gladiador
governor	gobernador

honor	honor
horror	**horror**
humor	humor *(also used for "mood" and "temper")*
illuminator	iluminador
illustrator	ilustrador
imitator	imitador
impostor	impostor
improvisor	improvisador
incinerator	incinerador
indicator	indicador
inferior	**inferior** *(also used for "lower")*
initiator	iniciador
innovator	**innovador**
inspector	inspector
instigator	instigador
instructor	instructor
interceptor	interceptor
interior	**interior**
interlocutor	interlocutor
interrogator	interrogador
interruptor	interruptor *(also used for "electrical switch")*
inventor	**inventor**
"Thomas Edison was an inventor."	**"Thomas Edison fue inventor".**
investigator	investigador
laminator	laminador
legislator	legislador
liberator	libertador
liquidator	liquidador
liquor	licor
major	mayor *(meaning "bigger" or "older")*

manipulator	manipulador
matador	matador
mediator	mediador
mentor	mentor
minor	menor *(also used for "smaller" or "younger")*
mitigator	mitigador
moderator	moderador
monitor	monitor
motor	**motor**
multicolor	multicolor
narrator	narrador
navigator	navegador *(more commonly "navegante")*
negotiator	negociador
odor	**olor** *(also used for "scent")*
operator	operador
oppressor	opresor
orator	orador
pastor	pastor
persecutor	perseguidor
possessor	poseedor
posterior	posterior
preceptor	preceptor
precursor	precursor
predator	depredador
predecessor	predecesor
processor	procesador
procreator	procreador
professor	**profesor** *(also used for "teacher")*
projector	proyector
propagator	propagador
protector	**protector**

radiator	radiador
rancor	rencor
raptor	raptor
reactor	reactor
receptor	receptor
rector	rector
reflector	reflector
refrigerator	refrigerador
regulator	regulador
renovator	renovador
repressor	represor
respirator	respirador
resuscitator	resucitador
rigor	rigor
rotor	rotor
rumor	rumor *(also used for "murmur")*
savior	salvador
sculptor	escultor
sector	sector
selector	selector
semiconductor	semiconductor
senator	**senador**
sensor	sensor
separator	separador
simulator	simulador
spectator	espectador
speculator	especulador
splendor	esplendor
stupor	estupor
successor	sucesor
superior	superior *(also used for "upper")*
supervisor	supervisor
suppressor	supresor
technicolor	tecnicolor

tenor . . . . tenor
terminator. . . . . terminador
terror . . . . **terror**
tractor . . . . tractor
traitor. . . . . traidor
transgressor . . . . transgresor
transistor . . . . transistor
translator . . . . traductor
tremor . . . . temblor
tricolor . . . . tricolor
tumor. . . . . **tumor**
    "It's a benign tumor." . . . . **"Es un tumor benigno".**
tutor. . . . . tutor *(also used for "guardian")*

ulterior . . . . ulterior

valor . . . . valor
vapor. . . . . **vapor**
vector. . . . . vector
vendor . . . . vendedor
ventilator . . . . ventilador *(meaning "electric fan")*
violator. . . . . violador *(also used for "rapist")*
vibrator . . . . vibrador
vigor . . . . vigor

18A.

Una las palabras que están relacionadas o que son sinónimos.

1. motor	gracias
2. color	afuera
3. favor	coche
4. terror	libro
5. autor	patente
6. inventor	horror
7. exterior	verde

18B.

Escuche y lea el cuento. Responda las siguientes preguntas, usando oraciones completas.

Apenas llegan a Córdoba, el tío les dice que habrá una fiesta en su casa esa noche. Angélica nota inmediatamente el _terror_ en la cara de Juan. Cuando están sólos, Juan dice, "¡Qué _error_ venir aquí! Hazme un _favor_ y dime que no tengo que ir (I don't have to go) **a esa fiesta". Angélica ni siquiera responde** (doesn't even respond) **y Juan comprende que debe ir. La "fiesta" es muy difícil para Juan. Cada dos minutos, el tío dice, "Aquel hombre es _doctor_, aquel allá es _profesor_, el otro es _inventor_". Por un momentito Juan se interesa** (he's interested) **cuando el tío dice, "El _senador_ va a venir con un _actor_ muy famoso". Pero el _actor_ no es famoso y el _senador_ es muy, muy viejo.**

1. ¿Qué nota Angélica en la cara de Juan?

2. ¿Qué dice Juan sobre la decisión de ir a Córdoba?

3. ¿Qué dice Juan sobre la fiesta?

4. ¿El actor es famoso?

5. ¿El senador es joven?

Chapter 19

English words ending in "–ory" generally correspond to "–orio" in Spanish.

Spanish words ending in "–orio" are usually adjectives or masculine nouns. For example,

> contradictory (adj.) = *contradictorio*
> laboratory (n.) = *el laboratorio*

ENGLISH . . . . SPANISH

*All words and phrases in bold are on **Track 19** of the accompanying CD.*

accessory . . . . **accesorio**
   "She's buying an accessory." . . . **"Ella compra un accesorio".**
accusatory . . . . acusatorio
ambulatory . . . . ambulatorio
anti-inflammatory . . . . antiinflammatorio

circulatory . . . . circulatorio
combinatory . . . . combinatorio
compensatory . . . . compensatorio
conservatory . . . . conservatorio
contradictory . . . . **contradictorio**
   "It's a contradictory response." . . . **"Es una respuesta contradictoria".**
crematory . . . . crematorio

defamatory . . . . difamatorio
directory . . . . directorio
discriminatory . . . . discriminatorio
dormitory . . . . dormitorio

illusory . . . . ilusorio

inflammatory. . . . . inflamatorio
introductory . . . . introductorio

laboratory . . . . **laboratorio**
lavatory . . . . lavatorio

migratory . . . . migratorio

obligatory . . . . **obligatorio**
observatory . . . . observatorio
oratory. . . . . oratorio

peremptory. . . . . perentorio
predatory. . . . . depredatorio
preparatory . . . . preparatorio
promissory . . . . promisorio
promontory. . . . . promontorio
provisory . . . . provisorio *(more commonly
"provisional")*

purgatory. . . . . **purgatorio**
   "Dante wrote about   **"Dante escribió del
    purgatory."**. . . . . **purgatorio".**

reformatory. . . . . reformatorio
repertory . . . . repertorio
repository. . . . . repositorio
respiratory . . . . respiratorio

satisfactory. . . . . satisfactorio
suppository. . . . . supositorio

territory . . . . **territorio**
transitory . . . . transitorio

unsatisfactory . . . . insatisfactorio

19A.

Una las palabras que están relacionadas o que son sinónimos.

1. accesorio   zona
2. territorio   aretes
3. dormitorio   telescopio
4. laboratorio   insulto
5. observatorio   prólogo
6. derogatorio   experimento
7. introductorio   cama

19B.

Escuche y lea el cuento. Responda las siguientes preguntas, usando oraciones completas.

Juan está muy contento cuando finalmente parten de Córdoba hacia Sevilla. Dice, "Hubiera preferido (I'd have preferred) **un hostal". Angélica admite que fue un <u>territorio</u> extraño. Juan dice, "Pero, ¿qué dices? ¡Fue peor que el <u>purgatorio</u>!" Angélica responde, "No tenías que** (you didn't have to) **venir, no era <u>obligatorio</u>". Juan se ríe de ese comentario <u>contradictorio</u> pero no responde. Juan dice, "Entonces me debes** (you owe me) **un favor, ¿verdad?" Angélica dice, "Veremos...".**

1. ¿Adónde van después de Córdoba?

2. ¿Qué hubiera preferido Juan?

3. Juan dice que la fiesta fue peor que ¿qué?

4. ¿Es verdad que su presencia (his presence) no era obligatoria?

5. ¿Responde Juan al último comentario contradictorio de Angélica?

Chapter 20

English words ending in "–ous" generally correspond to "–oso" in Spanish.

Spanish words ending in "–oso" are usually adjectives. For example,

> a <u>generous</u> gift = *un regalo <u>generoso</u>*

ENGLISH . . . . SPANISH

*All words and phrases in bold are on **Track 20** of the accompanying CD.*

advantageous . . . . ventajoso
ambitious . . . . **ambicioso**
amorous . . . . amoroso
anxious . . . . ansioso

calamitous . . . . calamitoso
callous . . . . calloso
cancerous . . . . canceroso
capricious . . . . caprichoso
cavernous . . . . cavernoso
ceremonious . . . . ceremonioso
clamorous . . . . clamoroso
contagious . . . . contagioso
copious . . . . copioso
curious . . . . **curioso**

decorous . . . . decoroso
delicious . . . . **delicioso**
    "The food is delicious." . . . . . **"La comida es deliciosa".**
desirous . . . . deseoso
disadvantageous . . . . desventajoso
disastrous . . . . **desastroso**

dubious	dudoso
envious	envidioso
fabulous	fabuloso
famous	famoso
fastidious	fastidioso *(meaning "annoying")*
fibrous	fibroso
furious	**furioso**
gaseous	gaseoso
gelatinous	gelatinoso
generous	**generoso**

"She is very generous." . . . . . **"Ella es muy generosa".**

glamorous	glamoroso
glorious	glorioso
gracious	gracioso *(meaning "funny")*
harmonious	armonioso
ignominious	ignominioso
impetuous	impetuoso
incestuous	incestuoso
indecorous	indecoroso
industrious	industrioso
ingenious	ingenioso
insidious	insidioso
jealous	celoso
joyous	jubiloso
judicious	juicioso
laborious	laborioso
litigious	litigioso
luminous	luminoso
luxurious	lujoso

INSTANT Spanish Vocabulary Builder

malicious . . . . malicioso
marvelous. . . . . maravilloso
melodious. . . . . melodioso
meticulous. . . . . meticuloso
miraculous . . . . milagroso
monstrous . . . . monstruoso
mucous. . . . . mucoso
mysterious . . . . **misterioso**

nebulous. . . . . nebuloso
nervous . . . . **nervioso**
  "Are you nervous?" . . . . **"¿Estás nervioso?"**
numerous . . . . numeroso

obsequious. . . . . obsequioso
odious . . . . odioso
onerous . . . . oneroso
ostentatious. . . . . ostentoso

perilous . . . . peligroso
pernicious. . . . . pernicioso
pious . . . . piadoso
pompous . . . . pomposo
populous . . . . populoso
porous . . . . poroso
portentous . . . . portentoso
precious . . . . **precioso**
prestigious . . . . **prestigioso**
presumptuous . . . . presuntuoso
pretentious . . . . pretencioso
prodigious . . . . prodigioso

rancorous . . . . rencoroso
religious . . . . **religioso**
rigorous . . . . riguroso
ruinous. . . . . ruinoso

scabrous	escabroso
scandalous	**escandaloso**
scrupulous	escrupuloso
semiprecious	semiprecioso
sinuous	sinuoso
spacious	**espacioso**
studious	estudioso
sumptuous	suntuoso
superstitious	supersticioso
suspicious	sospechoso
tedious	tedioso
tempestuous	tempestuoso
tortuous	**tortuoso**
"The trip was tortuous."	**"El viaje fue tortuoso".**
tumultuous	tumultuoso
vaporous	vaporoso
vicious	vicioso *(meaning "depraved," or "addicted")*
victorious	victorioso
vigorous	vigoroso
virtuous	**virtuoso**
viscous	viscoso
voluminous	voluminoso
voluptuous	voluptuoso

20A.

Una las palabras que están relacionadas o que son sinónimos.

1. curioso	enojado
2. famoso	amplio
3. delicioso	suspenso
4. misterioso	sabroso
5. furioso	inquisitivo
6. precioso	diamante
7. espacioso	celebridad

20B.

Escuche y lea el cuento. Responda las siguientes preguntas, usando oraciones completas.

Después de la visita <u>desastrosa</u> a Córdoba, los dos viajeros están listos para un fin de semana <u>ambicioso</u> en Sevilla. Angélica sabe que este lugar (this place) **es <u>famoso</u> por los churros <u>deliciosos</u>, pero no sabe mucho más de la ciudad. Juan también está muy <u>curioso</u> por conocer a Sevilla. Su amigo le dijo** (told him) **que hay un aire <u>misterioso</u> allí. En la Universidad de Sevilla hay un programa <u>famoso</u> de lenguas extranjeras. Angélica dice, "Cualquiera que estudie** (whoever studies) **en el extranjero debe ser <u>ambicioso</u>". Están en un hotel muy <u>espacioso</u>, y se encuentran muy bien allí. Antes de partir para Toledo, Angélica dice, "Me gusta mucho Sevilla, pero no es un lugar <u>misterioso</u>, ¡tal vez tu amigo es un tipo <u>nervioso</u>!"**

1. ¿Qué tipo de fin de semana quieren pasar en Sevilla?

2. ¿Por qué es famosa Sevilla?

3. ¿Qué dijo el amigo de Juan sobre esta ciudad?

4. ¿Cuál es el programa famoso en la Universidad de Sevilla?

5. ¿Cómo es su hotel?

-sion/-sión

English words ending in "–sion" generally correspond to "–sión" in Spanish.

Spanish words ending in "–sión" are usually feminine nouns. For example,

an explosion = *una explosión*

ENGLISH . . . . SPANISH	
abrasion	abrasión
adhesion	adhesión
admission	admisión
aggression	agresión
allusion	alusión
apprehension	aprehensión
ascension	ascensión
aversion	aversión
circumcision	circuncisión
cohesion	cohesión
collision	**colisión**
"There was a collision."	**"Hubo una colisión".**
collusion	colusión
commission	comisión
compassion	compasión
comprehension	**comprensión**
compression	compresión
compulsion	compulsión
concession	concesión
conclusion	**conclusión**
confession	confesión

All words and phrases in bold are on **Track 21** *of the accompanying CD.*

confusion	**confusión**
contusion	contusión
conversion	conversión
convulsion	convulsión
corrosion	corrosión
decision	**decisión**
decompression	descompresión
depression	depresión
diffusion	difusión
digression	digresión
dimension	**dimensión**
discussion	discusión *(meaning "argument")*
disillusion	desilusión *(also used for "disappointment")*
dispersion	dispersión
dissension	disensión
dissuasion	disuasión
diversion	diversión
division	**división**
effusion	efusión
emission	emisión
emulsion	emulsión
erosion	erosión
evasion	evasión *(also used for "escape")*
exclusion	exclusión
excursion	excursión
expansion	expansión
explosion	**explosión**
expression	**expresión**
"Another idiomatic expression!"	**"¡Otra expresión idiomática!"**
expulsion	expulsión
extension	extensión
extroversion	extroversión

fission . . . . fisión
fusion . . . . fusión *(also used for "merger")*

hypertension . . . . hipertensión

illusion . . . . ilusión
immersion . . . . inmersión
implosion . . . . implosión
imprecision . . . . imprecisión
impression . . . . **impresión** *(also used for "printing")*
incision . . . . incisión
inclusion . . . . inclusión
incomprehension . . . . incomprensión
indecision . . . . indecisión
infusion . . . . infusión
intercession . . . . intercesión
intermission . . . . intermisión *(for shows/theater,*
use "entreacto")

introversion . . . . introversión
intrusion . . . . intrusión
invasion . . . . invasión
inversion . . . . inversión

lesion . . . . lesión

mansion . . . . mansión
mission . . . . **misión**

obsession . . . . obsesión
occasion . . . . ocasión *(also used for "opportunity")*
occlusion . . . . oclusión
omission . . . . omisión
oppression . . . . opresión

passion . . . . **pasión**
    "I have a passion for   **"Siento pasión por**
    Spanish." . . . . **el español".**
pension . . . . pensión *(also used for "small hotel")*
percussion . . . . percusión
persuasion . . . . persuasión
perversion . . . . perversión
possession . . . . posesión
precision. . . . . **precisión**
pretension. . . . . pretensión
prevision . . . . previsión
procession . . . . procesión
profession. . . . . **profesión**
profusion . . . . profusión
progression. . . . . progresión
propulsion . . . . propulsión
provision . . . . provisión

recession . . . . recesión
reclusion. . . . . reclusión
regression. . . . . regresión
remission . . . . remisión
repercussion . . . . repercusión
reprehension. . . . . reprensión
repression. . . . . represión
repulsion . . . . repulsión
reversion . . . . reversión
revision . . . . revisión
revulsion. . . . . revulsión *(only used in a medical context)*

secession . . . . secesión
session . . . . **sesión**
subdivision . . . . subdivisión
submersion . . . . inmersión
submission . . . . sumisión

subversion . . . . subversión
succession . . . . sucesión
supervision . . . . supervisión
suppression. . . . . supresión
suspension . . . . suspensión

television . . . . **televisión**
    "Let's watch television." . . . . . **"Miremos la televisión"**.
tension . . . . **tensión**
transfusion . . . . transfusión
transgression. . . . . transgresión
transmission . . . . transmisión

version . . . . versión
vision . . . . **visión**

21A.

Una las palabras que están relacionadas o que son sinónimos.

1.	confusión	caos
2.	misión	bomba
3.	televisión	antena
4.	explosión	objetivo
5.	pasión	ojo
6.	precisión	exactitud
7.	visión	amor

21B.

Escuche y lea el cuento. Responda las siguientes preguntas, usando oraciones completas.

Apenas llegan a Toledo, Angélica declara, "Tenemos una <u>misión</u> clara aquí en Toledo. Tú sabes que la cerámica es una <u>pasión</u> mía, ¿verdad? Tengo que encontrar (I must find) un plato de cerámica nuevo para mi colección". Juan dice, "Está bien, pero ¿tal vez lo podemos encontrar en La Coruña?" Angélica insiste, "¡NO! ¡Mi <u>decisión</u> es final! Quiero un plato de Toledo". Juan tiene la <u>impresión</u> de que Angélica no está bromeando (isn't kidding around), y él se dedica a la "<u>misión</u> del plato". Después de un almuerzo fabuloso en la plaza ellos comienzan la caza (the hunt). Había un poco de <u>confusión</u> con todas las callejuelas y callejones, pero al final hay una <u>conclusión</u> feliz— Angélica encuentra su plato.

1. ¿Cuál es la misión de Angélica?

2. ¿Por qué quiere eso?

3. ¿Qué dice Angélica de su decisión?

4. ¿Qué impresión tiene Juan de Angélica?

5. ¿Por qué había un poco de confusión?

-sis/-sis

English words ending in "–sis" often have the same ending in Spanish.

Spanish words ending in "–sis" are usually nouns. For example,

an analysis = *un análisis*

ENGLISH . . . . SPANISH

*All words and phrases in bold are on **Track 22** of the accompanying CD.*

analysis . . . . **análisis**
antithesis . . . . antítesis

biogenesis . . . . biogénesis

catalysis . . . . catálisis
catharsis. . . . . catarsis
chassis . . . . chasís
cirrhosis . . . . cirrosis
crisis . . . . **crisis**

diagnosis . . . . diagnosis
dialysis. . . . . **diálisis**

electrolysis . . . . electrólisis
emphasis . . . . **énfasis**
    "You need more emphasis." . . . **"Necesitas más énfasis"**.

fibrosis. . . . . fibrosis

genesis. . . . . **génesis**

halitosis . . . . halitosis
hydrolysis . . . . hidrólisis
hypnosis . . . . **hipnosis**
hypothesis . . . . **hipótesis**
  "What is your hypothesis?" . . . **"¿Cúal es tu hipótesis?"**

macroanalysis . . . . macroanálisis
metamorphosis . . . . **metamorfosis**
metastasis . . . . metástasis
microanalysis . . . . microanálisis
mononucleosis . . . . mononucleosis

narcosis . . . . narcosis
nemesis . . . . némesis
neurosis . . . . neurosis

oasis . . . . oasis
osmosis . . . . ósmosis
osteoporosis . . . . osteoporosis

paralysis . . . . parálisis
parenthesis . . . . paréntesis
photogenesis . . . . fotogénesis
photosynthesis . . . . fotosíntesis
prognosis . . . . prognosis
prosthesis . . . . prótesis
psoriasis . . . . psoriasis
psychoanalysis . . . . psicoanálisis
psychosis . . . . psicosis

sclerosis . . . . esclerosis
scoliosis . . . . escoliosis
self-analysis . . . . autoanálisis
synopsis . . . . sinopsis
synthesis . . . . síntesis

thesis . . . . **tesis**

    "Did he write his thesis?" . . . . **"¿Él escribió la tesis?"**

tuberculosis . . . . tuberculosis

22A.

Una las palabras que están relacionadas o que son sinónimos.

1. crisis	soñar
2. tuberculosis	enfermedad
3. énfasis	cambio
4. parálisis	dificultad
5. hipnosis	inmovilidad
6. metamorfosis	acento
7. análisis	estudio

22B.

Escuche y lea el cuento. Responda las siguientes preguntas, usando oraciones completas.

Destinación: ¡Madrid! Juan y Angélica ya conocen a (already know) **Madrid bastante bien. Entonces no ponen mucho <u>énfasis</u> en el giro turístico. Van a buscar, en cambio, a un primo de Juan que estudia en Madrid. Se llama Carlos y estudia economía. Escribe su <u>tesis</u> sobre la <u>crisis</u> financiera del tercer mundo** (of the Third World)**. Juan y Angélica cenan en casa de Carlos y escuchan mientras Carlos habla largo y tendido sobre su <u>análisis</u> de la <u>crisis</u>. Carlos dice, "Desafortunadamente, no tengo una <u>hipótesis</u> propia sobre cómo mejorar** (to improve) **la <u>crisis</u>, y sin esta <u>hipótesis</u> ¡no puedo hacer mi <u>tesis</u>!" Carlos pregunta a Juan, "¿Puedes ayudarme?" Juan responde, "Veremos…".**

INSTANT Spanish Vocabulary Builder

1. ¿Por qué no ponen mucho énfasis en el giro turístico en Madrid?

2. ¿Sobre qué escribe la tesis Carlos?

3. ¿Carlos habla mucho sobre su análisis?

4. ¿Tiene Carlos una buena hipótesis para su tesis?

5. ¿Qué pregunta Carlos a Juan?

-tion/-ción

English words that end in "–tion" often correspond to "–ción" in Spanish.

Spanish words ending in "–ción" are usually feminine nouns. For example,

an operation = *una operación*

ENGLISH . . . . SPANISH	

*All words and phrases in bold are on **Track 23** of the accompanying CD.*

abbreviation . . . . abreviación *(meaning "a shortening")*

abdication . . . . abdicación

aberration . . . . aberración

abolition . . . . abolición

abomination . . . . abominación

absolution . . . . absolución

absorption . . . . absorción

abstention . . . . abstención

abstraction . . . . abstracción

acceleration . . . . aceleración

acclamation . . . . aclamación

accommodation . . . . acomodación *(more commonly "alojamiento," for lodging)*

accreditation . . . . acreditación

acculturation . . . . aculturación

accumulation . . . . acumulación

accusation . . . . acusación

acquisition . . . . adquisición

action . . . . **acción** *(also used for "stock share")*

"There's not a lot of action." . . . **"No hay mucha acción".**

activation . . . . activación

actualization . . . . actualización

adaptation . . . . adaptación

addiction . . . . adicción

addition . . . . adición

administration . . . . administración

admiration . . . . admiración

admonition . . . . admonición

adoption . . . . adopción

adoration . . . . adoración

adulation . . . . adulación

adulteration . . . . adulteración

affiliation . . . . afiliación

affirmation . . . . afirmación

affliction . . . . aflicción

agitation . . . . agitación

alienation . . . . alienación

alliteration . . . . aliteración

alteration . . . . alteración

ambition . . . . **ambición**

    "They have ambition." . . . . . . **"Tienen ambición".**

Americanization . . . . americanización

amputation . . . . amputación

animation . . . . animación

annotation . . . . anotación

anticipation . . . . anticipación

apparition . . . . aparición

application . . . . aplicación *(for "application form," use "solicitud")*

appreciation . . . . apreciación

approbation . . . . aprobación

approximation . . . . aproximación

aspiration . . . . aspiración

assimilation . . . . asimilación

association . . . . asociación

attention . . . . **atención** *(also used for "attention please!")*

INSTANT Spanish Vocabulary Builder

attenuation . . . . atenuación

attraction . . . . atracción

attribution . . . . atribución

audition . . . . audición

authentication . . . . autenticación

authorization . . . . autorización

automation . . . . automatización

aviation . . . . aviación *(also used for "air force")*

benediction . . . . bendición

cancellation . . . . cancelación

capitalization . . . . capitalización

celebration . . . . celebración

    "It's a big celebration." . . . . . **"Es una gran celebración".**

centralization . . . . centralización

certification . . . . certificación

circulation . . . . circulación

citation . . . . citación

civilization . . . . civilización

classification . . . . clasificación

coaction . . . . coacción

coalition . . . . coalición

codification . . . . codificación

cognition . . . . cognición

cohabitation . . . . cohabitación

collaboration . . . . colaboración

collection . . . . colección

colonization . . . . colonización

coloration . . . . coloración

combination . . . . combinación

commemoration . . . . conmemoración

commiseration . . . . conmiseración

commotion . . . . conmoción

communication . . . . comunicación

compensation . . . . compensación

competition	competición
compilation	compilación
complication	complicación
composition	composición
concentration	concentración
conception	concepción
condensation	condensación
condition	**condición**
conduction	conducción *(also used for "the act of guiding")*
confection	confección *(meaning "the making of")*
confederation	confederación
confirmation	confirmación
confiscation	confiscación
conformation	conformación
confrontation	confrontación
congregation	congregación
conjugation	conjugación
conjunction	conjunción
connotation	connotación
conservation	conservación
consideration	consideración
consolation	consolación
consolidation	consolidación
constellation	constelación
consternation	consternación
constipation	constipación *(meaning "head congestion")*
constitution	constitución
constriction	constricción
construction	construcción
consummation	consumación
contamination	contaminación *(also used for "pollution")*
contemplation	contemplación
contention	contención *(meaning "retention")*
continuation	continuación

INSTANT Spanish Vocabulary Builder

contraction . . . . contracción
contradiction . . . . contradicción
contribution . . . . contribución
contrition . . . . contrición
convention . . . . convención
conversation . . . . **conversación**
conviction . . . . convicción
cooperation . . . . cooperación
coordination . . . . **coordinación**
coproduction . . . . coproducción
coronation . . . . coronación
corporation . . . . corporación
correction . . . . corrección
correlation . . . . correlación
corruption . . . . corrupción
creation . . . . creación
cremation . . . . cremación
crystallization . . . . cristalización
culmination . . . . culminación
cumulation . . . . acumulación

decapitation . . . . decapitación
deceleration . . . . desaceleración
decentralization . . . . descentralización
deception . . . . decepción *(meaning "disappointment")*
declamation . . . . declamación
declaration . . . . declaración
declination . . . . declinación
decomposition . . . . descomposición
decoration . . . . decoración
dedication . . . . dedicación
deduction . . . . deducción
defamation . . . . difamación
definition . . . . **definición**
deflation . . . . deflación *(only used in an economic context)*

deforestation . . . . desforestación

deformation . . . . deformación

degeneration . . . . degeneración

degradation . . . . degradación

dehumanization . . . . deshumanización

dehydration . . . . deshidratación

delegation . . . . delegación

deliberation . . . . deliberación

delimitation. . . . . delimitación

demarcation . . . . demarcación

demolition . . . . demolición

demonstration . . . . demostración

denomination . . . . denominación

deportation. . . . . deportación

depravation . . . . depravación

depreciation . . . . depreciación

description . . . . descripción

desertion . . . . deserción

desolation. . . . . desolación

desperation. . . . . desesperación

destabilization . . . . desestabilización

destination . . . . destinación

destitution. . . . . destitución *(meaning "dismissal")*

destruction . . . . **destrucción**

detention . . . . detención

determination . . . . determinación

devastation. . . . . devastación

deviation . . . . desviación

devotion. . . . . devoción

diction . . . . dicción

differentiation . . . . diferenciación

digestion . . . . digestión

direction. . . . . **dirección** *(also used for*
"street address")

discretion . . . . discreción

discrimination . . . . discriminación

disfunction . . . . disfunción
disintegration . . . . desintegración
disorganization . . . . desorganización
disorientation . . . . desorientación
disposition . . . . disposición
disproportion . . . . desproporción
disqualification . . . . descalificación
dissection . . . . disección
dissertation . . . . disertación
distillation . . . . destilación
distinction . . . . distinción
distraction . . . . distracción
distribution . . . . distribución
diversification . . . . diversificación
documentation . . . . documentación
domination . . . . dominación
donation . . . . donación
dramatization . . . . dramatización
duplication . . . . duplicación
duration . . . . duración

edition . . . . **edición**
    "It's a new edition." . . . . **"Es una nueva edición".**
education . . . . educación *(also used for "manners")*
ejection . . . . eyección *(more commonly "expulsión")*
elaboration . . . . elaboración
election . . . . elección
electrocution . . . . electrocución
elevation . . . . elevación
elimination . . . . eliminación
elocution . . . . elocución
emancipation . . . . emancipación
embarcation . . . . embarcación *(meaning "boat")*
emigration . . . . emigración
emotion . . . . **emoción**
emulation . . . . emulación

enunciation . . . . enunciación

equation . . . . ecuación

erection . . . . erección

erudition . . . . erudición

eruption . . . . erupción

evaluation . . . . evaluación

evaporation . . . . evaporación

evolution . . . . evolución

exaggeration . . . . **exageración**

examination . . . . examinación *(more commonly "examen")*

exasperation . . . . exasperación

excavation . . . . excavación

exception . . . . excepción

exclamation . . . . exclamación

excretion . . . . excreción

execution . . . . ejecución

exhibition . . . . exhibición

exhortation . . . . exhortación

expedition . . . . expedición

exploration . . . . exploración

exportation . . . . exportación

exposition . . . . exposición

extinction . . . . extinción

extraction . . . . extracción

extradition . . . . extradición

exultation . . . . exultación

fabrication . . . . fabricación *(meaning "manufacturing")*

falsification . . . . falsificación

federation . . . . federación

fermentation . . . . fermentación

fertilization . . . . fertilización

fiction . . . . ficción

filtration . . . . filtración

finalization . . . . finalización

fixation . . . . fijación

fluctuation. . . . . fluctuación

formation . . . . formación *(also used for "training")*

formulation . . . . formulación

fossilization. . . . . fosilización

foundation . . . . **fundación**

fraction . . . . fracción

fragmentation . . . . fragmentación

friction . . . . fricción

fruition . . . . fruición

frustration . . . . frustración

fumigation . . . . fumigación

function . . . . función

generalization. . . . . generalización

generation . . . . **generación**

"Every generation changes." . . . **"Cada generación cambia"**.

germination . . . . germinación

gestation . . . . gestación

globalization. . . . . globalización

glorification . . . . glorificación

graduation . . . . graduación

gratification . . . . gratificación *(also used for "tip")*

gravitation . . . . gravitación

habitation. . . . . habitación *(meaning "bedroom")*

hallucination . . . . alucinación

humiliation . . . . humillación

identification. . . . . identificación

ignition. . . . . ignición

illumination . . . . iluminación

illustration. . . . . ilustración

imagination . . . . imaginación

imitation . . . . **imitación**

"It's a horrible imitation!" . . . . **"¡Es una mala imitación!"**

immigration . . . . inmigración

imperfection . . . . imperfección

implication . . . . implicación

importation . . . . importación

improvisation . . . . improvisación

inaction . . . . inacción

inauguration . . . . inauguración

incarnation . . . . encarnación

incineration . . . . incineración

inclination . . . . inclinación

incrimination . . . . incriminación

incubation . . . . incubación

indignation . . . . indignación

indiscretion . . . . indiscreción

induction . . . . inducción

infatuation . . . . infatuación *(meaning "vanity")*

infection . . . . infección

infiltration . . . . infiltración

inflamation . . . . inflamación

inflation . . . . inflación

information . . . . **información**

inhibition . . . . inhibición

initiation . . . . iniciación

injection . . . . inyección

innovation . . . . innovación

inquisition . . . . inquisición

inscription . . . . inscripción *(also used for "enrollment," "registration")*

insemination . . . . inseminación

insertion . . . . inserción

inspection . . . . inspección

inspiration . . . . inspiración

installation . . . . instalación

institution . . . . institución

instruction . . . . instrucción
insurrection . . . . insurrección
integration . . . . integración
intensification . . . . intensificación
intention . . . . **intención**
interaction . . . . interacción
interception . . . . interceptación
interpretation . . . . interpretación
interrogation . . . . interrogación
interruption . . . . interrupción
intersection . . . . intersección
intervention . . . . intervención *(also used for "surgery")*
intimidation . . . . intimidación
intonation . . . . entonación
intoxication . . . . intoxicación *(meaning "poisoning")*
introduction . . . . introducción
introspection . . . . introspección
intuition . . . . intuición
inundation . . . . inundación
invention . . . . **invención**
investigation . . . . investigación
invitation . . . . invitación
irrigation . . . . irrigación
irritation . . . . irritación *(also used for "rash")*

justification . . . . justificación
juxtaposition . . . . yuxtaposición

lamination . . . . laminación
legalization . . . . legalización
legislation . . . . legislación
levitation . . . . levitación
liberation . . . . liberación
limitation . . . . limitación
liposuction . . . . liposucción
liquidation . . . . liquidación

Chapter 23

litigation . . . . litigación
location . . . . localización
locomotion . . . . locomoción
lotion . . . . **loción**
    "We don't have any more lotion." . . . **"No tenemos más loción"**.
lubrication . . . . lubricación

malformation . . . . malformación
malnutrition . . . . malnutrición
manifestation . . . . manifestación *(also used for*
                                     "public demonstration")
manipulation . . . . manipulación
masturbation . . . . masturbación
maturation . . . . maduración
medication . . . . medicación
meditation . . . . meditación
memorization . . . . memorización
menstruation . . . . menstruación
mention . . . . mención
migration . . . . migración
mitigation . . . . mitigación
moderation . . . . moderación
modification . . . . modificación
modulation . . . . modulación
monopolization . . . . monopolización
motion . . . . moción *(meaning "proposal")*
motivation . . . . motivación
multiplication . . . . multiplicación
mutation . . . . mutación

narration . . . . narración
nation . . . . **nación**
navigation . . . . navegación
negation . . . . negación
negotiation . . . . negociación
nomination . . . . nominación

notation . . . . notación
notion . . . . noción
nutrition . . . . nutrición

objection . . . . objeción
obligation. . . . . obligación
observation. . . . . observación
obstruction . . . . obstrucción
occupation . . . . ocupación
operation . . . . **operación**
    "She needs an operation." . . . **"Ella necesita una operación"**.
opposition . . . . oposición
option . . . . opción
oration . . . . oración
organization . . . . organización
orientation . . . . orientación
ovulation . . . . ovulación
oxidation . . . . oxidación

pagination . . . . paginación
palpitation . . . . palpitación
participation . . . . participación
partition . . . . partición
penetration . . . . penetración
perception . . . . percepción
perfection . . . . perfección
perforation . . . . perforación
perpetuation . . . . perpetuación
persecution . . . . persecución
personalization . . . . personalización
personification . . . . personificación
petition. . . . . petición
pollution. . . . . polución
population . . . . **población**
portion. . . . . porción

position . . . . **posición** *(for employment,*
use "puesto")

"What is his/her position?" . . . **"¿Cúal es su posición?"**

postproduction . . . . posproducción
postulation . . . . postulación
potion . . . . poción
precaution . . . . precaución
precipitation . . . . precipitación
precondition . . . . precondición
predestination . . . . predestinación
prediction . . . . predicción
predilection . . . . predilección
predisposition . . . . predisposición
premeditation . . . . premeditación
premonition . . . . premonición
preoccupation . . . . **preocupación**
preparation . . . . preparación
preposition . . . . preposición
prescription . . . . prescripción
presentation . . . . presentación
preservation . . . . preservación
presumption . . . . presunción
prevention . . . . prevención
privation . . . . privación
privatization . . . . privatización
proclamation . . . . proclamación
procreation . . . . procreación
production . . . . producción
prohibition . . . . prohibición
projection . . . . proyección
proliferation . . . . proliferación
promotion . . . . promoción
pronunciation . . . . pronunciación
proportion . . . . proporción
proposition . . . . proposición
prostitution . . . . prostitución

INSTANT Spanish Vocabulary Builder

protection . . . . protección
provocation . . . . provocación
publication . . . . publicación
punctuation. . . . . puntuación
purification . . . . purificación

qualification . . . . cualificación
quantification . . . . cuantificación

radiation . . . . radiación
ramification . . . . ramificación
ration. . . . . ración
reaction . . . . **reacción**
reactivation. . . . . reactivación
realization . . . . realización *(meaning "completion")*
reception . . . . recepción
recommendation . . . . recomendación
recollection . . . . recolección *(meaning "gathering")*
reconciliation . . . . reconciliación
recreation. . . . . recreación
recrimination. . . . . recriminación
recuperation . . . . recuperación
reduction . . . . reducción
reelection . . . . reelección
reevaluation . . . . reevaluación
refraction . . . . refracción
refrigeration . . . . refrigeración
regulation. . . . . regulación
rehabilitation. . . . . rehabilitación
reincarnation . . . . reencarnación
relation . . . . relación
relaxation. . . . . relajación
renovation . . . . renovación
reorganization . . . . reorganización
reparation . . . . reparación
repetition . . . . repetición

reproduction . . . . reproducción

reputation . . . . **reputación**

    "He has a good reputation." . . . **"Él tiene una buena reputación"**.

reservation . . . . reservación

resignation . . . . resignación *(meaning "yielding";*
                                       "job resignation" is
                                       "dimisión")

resolution . . . . resolución

respiration . . . . respiración

restitution . . . . restitución

restoration . . . . restauración

restriction . . . . restricción

resurrection. . . . . resurrección

retention. . . . . retención

retraction . . . . retracción

retribution . . . . retribución

revelation . . . . revelación

revolution . . . . **revolución**

rotation . . . . rotación

salvation . . . . salvación

sanction . . . . sanción

satisfaction . . . . **satisfacción**

    "It gives me a lot of satisfaction." . . . **"Me da mucha satisfacción"**.

saturation . . . . saturación

secretion. . . . . secreción

section . . . . sección

sedation . . . . sedación

sedition . . . . sedición

seduction . . . . seducción

segmentation . . . . segmentación

segregation . . . . segregación

selection. . . . . selección

self-destruction. . . . . autodestrucción

sensation . . . . sensación

separation . . . . separación

simplification. . . . . simplificación

simulation. . . . . simulación

situation . . . . **situación**

solution . . . . **solución**

sophistication . . . . sofisticación

specialization . . . . especialización

specification . . . . especificación

speculation. . . . . especulación

stabilization . . . . estabilización

station . . . . **estación**

sterilization. . . . . esterilización

stimulation . . . . estimulación *(more commonly*
"estímulo")

stipulation. . . . . estipulación

sublimation. . . . . sublimación

subordination . . . . subordinación

substitution . . . . sustitución

subtraction . . . . sustracción

superstition . . . . superstición

supposition . . . . suposición

synchronization. . . . . sincronización

temptation . . . . tentación

termination . . . . terminación

tradition . . . . **tradición**

"It's a long tradition." . . . . . . **"Es una larga tradición".**

transaction . . . . transacción

transcription . . . . transcripción

transformation. . . . . transformación

transition . . . . transición

trepidation . . . . trepidación

tribulation. . . . . tribulación

unification . . . . unificación

vacation . . . . vacación

vacillation . . . . vacilación

validation . . . . validación

variation . . . . variación

vegetation . . . . vegetación

veneration . . . . veneración

ventilation . . . . ventilación

verification . . . . verificación

vibration . . . . vibración

vindication . . . . vindicación

violation . . . . violación

visualization . . . . visualización

vocalization . . . . vocalización

vocation . . . . vocación

23A.

Una las palabras que están relacionadas o que son sinónimos.

1. información	sentimiento
2. dirección	a la derecha
3. estación	fiesta
4. nación	noticias
5. emoción	país
6. solución	tren
7. celebración	resultado

23B.

Escuche y lea el cuento. Responda las siguientes preguntas, usando oraciones completas.

En la <u>estación</u> de Salamanca, Juan y Angélica ven un anuncio (a sign) **para una gran <u>celebración</u> en la plaza principal para esa noche. Leen la <u>información</u> y comprenden que esta fiesta será grande. Angélica no quiere ir porque no se siente bien** (she doesn't feel well)**. Juan dice, "Así me pagas el favor". Angélica ve que la <u>reacción</u> de Juan es fuerte y ella dice, "Está bien, vamos". Juan dice, "Pero qué <u>situación</u> perfecta para conocer esta bella ciudad y su cocina". La <u>reacción</u> de Angélica es más sobria** (subdued)**. Ella dice, "Sí, nos encontramos en una buena <u>posición</u> aquí". Al final de la fiesta Juan está más tranquilo. Él dice, "Angélica, comí y bebí demasiado, debo irme a dormir".**

1. ¿Dónde ven el anuncio para la celebración?

2. ¿Cómo será esta fiesta?

3. ¿Por qué es importante la celebración para Juan?

4. ¿Cómo es la reacción de Angélica?

5. Al final de la fiesta, ¿en qué condición se encuentra Juan?

INSTANT Spanish Vocabulary Builder

-ty/-dad

Many English words that end in "–ty" correspond to "–dad" in Spanish.

Spanish words ending in "–dad" are usually feminine nouns. For example,

the responsibility = *la responsabilidad*

ENGLISH . . . . SPANISH

*All words and phrases in bold are on **Track 24** of the accompanying CD.*

ability . . . . habilidad
abnormality . . . . anormalidad
acceptability . . . . aceptabilidad
accessibility . . . . accesibilidad
activity . . . . **actividad**
actuality . . . . actualidad *(meaning "current events")*
adaptability . . . . adaptabilidad
admissibility . . . . admisibilidad
adversity . . . . adversidad
affinity . . . . afinidad
aggressivity . . . . agresividad
agility . . . . agilidad
alacrity. . . . . alacridad
ambiguity . . . . ambigüedad
amenity . . . . amenidad
amorality . . . . amoralidad
animosity . . . . animosidad
annuity. . . . . anualidad
antiquity. . . . . antigüedad
anxiety. . . . . **ansiedad**
    "You have too much anxiety." . . . **"Tienes demasiada ansiedad"**.
applicability . . . . aplicabilidad

artificiality . . . . artificialidad
atrocity. . . . . atrocidad
austerity . . . . austeridad
authenticity . . . . autenticidad
authority . . . . autoridad

banality . . . . banalidad
barbarity . . . . barbaridad
bisexuality . . . . bisexualidad
brevity . . . . brevedad
brutality . . . . brutalidad

calamity . . . . calamidad
capacity . . . . capacidad
cavity . . . . cavidad *(for teeth, use "caries")*
celebrity . . . . **celebridad**
   "Paul Newman is   **"Paul Newman es una**
   a celebrity." . . . . **celebridad".**
centrality . . . . centralidad
charity . . . . caridad
chastity. . . . . castidad
Christianity . . . . Cristiandad
city . . . . ciudad
civility . . . . civilidad
clarity. . . . . claridad
collectivity. . . . . colectividad
commodity . . . . comodidad *(meaning "comfort,"*
                                                      "convenience")
communicability . . . . comunicabilidad
community . . . . **comunidad**
compatibility. . . . . compatibilidad
complexity . . . . complejidad
complicity. . . . . complicidad
conductivity . . . . conductividad
conformity . . . . conformidad
continuity . . . . continuidad

INSTANT Spanish Vocabulary Builder

cordiality . . . . cordialidad
corruptibility . . . . corruptibilidad
creativity . . . . **creatividad**
credibility . . . . credibilidad
cruelty . . . . crueldad
culpability. . . . . culpabilidad
curiosity . . . . **curiosidad**

debility. . . . . debilidad
deformity . . . . deformidad
density . . . . densidad
difficulty . . . . **dificultad**
dignity . . . . dignidad
discontinuity . . . . discontinuidad
dishonesty . . . . deshonestidad
disparity. . . . . disparidad
diversity . . . . diversidad
divinity. . . . . divinidad
divisibility . . . . divisibilidad
domesticity . . . . domesticidad
duality . . . . dualidad
duplicity . . . . duplicidad
durability . . . . durabilidad

elasticity . . . . elasticidad
electricity . . . . **electricidad**
    "There is no electricity." . . . . . **"No hay electricidad"**.
eligibility . . . . elegibilidad
enormity . . . . enormidad
entity . . . . entidad
equality . . . . igualdad
equanimity . . . . ecuanimidad
equity. . . . . equidad
eternity. . . . . eternidad
eventuality . . . . eventualidad
exclusivity. . . . . exclusividad

expressivity . . . . expresividad

extremity . . . . extremidad

facility . . . . facilidad *(meaning "talent" or "ease")*

faculty . . . . facultad *(only used for "university*
department," "right,"
or "ability")

fallibility . . . . falibilidad

falsity . . . . falsedad

familiarity . . . . familiaridad

fatality . . . . fatalidad *(also used for "misfortune,"*
"disaster")

felicity . . . . felicidad

femininity . . . . feminidad

ferocity . . . . ferocidad

fertility . . . . fertilidad

festivity . . . . festividad

fidelity . . . . fidelidad

finality . . . . finalidad *(meaning "goal,"*
"objective")

flexibility . . . . **flexibilidad**

"It's important
to have flexibility." . . . . **"Es importante**
tener flexibilidad".

formality . . . . formalidad

fragility . . . . fragilidad

fraternity . . . . fraternidad

frugality . . . . frugalidad

functionality . . . . funcionalidad

futility . . . . futilidad

generality . . . . generalidad

generosity . . . . **generosidad**

governability . . . . gobernabilidad

gratuity . . . . gratuidad *(meaning "free,"*
"no charge")

gravity . . . . gravedad

heterosexuality . . . . heterosexualidad
hilarity . . . . hilaridad
homosexuality . . . . homosexualidad
honesty . . . . honestidad
hospitality . . . . hospitalidad
hostility . . . . hostilidad
humanity . . . . humanidad
humidity . . . . humedad
humility . . . . humildad
hyperactivity . . . . hiperactividad

identity . . . . **identidad**
illegality . . . . ilegalidad
illegibility . . . . ilegibilidad
immensity . . . . inmensidad
immortality . . . . inmortalidad
immunity . . . . inmunidad
impartiality . . . . imparcialidad
Impassivity . . . . impasibilidad
impermeability . . . . impermeabilidad
impiety . . . . impiedad
impossibility . . . . **imposibilidad**
improbability . . . . improbabilidad
impropriety . . . . impropiedad
inactivity . . . . inactividad
incapacity . . . . incapacidad
incompatibility . . . . incompatibilidad
inconformity . . . . inconformidad
incredulity . . . . incredulidad
indignity . . . . indignidad
individuality . . . . individualidad
inequality . . . . desigualdad
inevitability . . . . inevitabilidad
infallibility . . . . infalibilidad
inferiority . . . . inferioridad
infertility . . . . infertilidad

infidelity . . . . infidelidad
infinity . . . . infinidad
infirmity . . . . enfermedad
inflexibility . . . . inflexibilidad
informality . . . . informalidad
ingenuity . . . . ingenuidad *(meaning "innocence,"*
"naiveté")

iniquity . . . . iniquidad
insecurity . . . . inseguridad
insensitivity . . . . insensibilidad
insincerity . . . . insinceridad
instability . . . . inestabilidad
integrity . . . . integridad
intensity . . . . **intensidad**
intolerability . . . . intolerabilidad
invariability . . . . invariabilidad
invisibility . . . . invisibilidad
invulnerability . . . . invulnerabilidad
irrationality . . . . irracionalidad
irregularity . . . . irregularidad
irresponsibility . . . . irresponsabilidad

legality . . . . legalidad
legibility . . . . legibilidad
liberty . . . . **libertad**
   "Here's the Statue   **"La Estatua de la Libertad**
     of Liberty." . . . . **está aquí".**
locality . . . . localidad
longevity . . . . longevidad
loyalty . . . . lealtad

magnanimity . . . . magnanimidad
majesty . . . . majestad
malleability . . . . maleabilidad
marginality . . . . marginalidad
masculinity . . . . masculinidad

INSTANT Spanish Vocabulary Builder

maternity . . . . maternidad
mediocrity . . . . mediocridad
mentality. . . . . mentalidad
mobility . . . . movilidad
modality. . . . . modalidad
modernity. . . . . modernidad
monstrosity . . . . monstruosidad
morality . . . . moralidad
mortality. . . . . mortalidad
multiplicity . . . . multiplicidad
mutability . . . . mutabilidad
mutuality. . . . . mutualidad
municipality . . . . municipalidad

Nativity . . . . Navidad *(meaning "Christmas")*
necessity. . . . . **necesidad**
negativity . . . . negatividad
neutrality . . . . neutralidad
normality . . . . normalidad
notoriety. . . . . notoriedad
novelty . . . . novedad

obesity . . . . obesidad
objectivity. . . . . objetividad
obscenity . . . . obscenidad
obscurity. . . . . oscuridad *(meaning "darkness")*
opportunity. . . . . **oportunidad**
originality. . . . . originalidad

parity. . . . . paridad
partiality. . . . . parcialidad
particularity . . . . particularidad
passivity . . . . pasividad
paternity. . . . . paternidad
peculiarity . . . . peculiaridad

penalty . . . . penalidad *(meaning "suffering,"*
"hardship")
permeability . . . . permeabilidad
permissibility . . . . permisibilidad
perpetuity . . . . perpetuidad
perplexity . . . . perplejidad
personality . . . . **personalidad**
perversity . . . . perversidad
piety . . . . piedad *(meaning "pity")*
plasticity . . . . plasticidad
plurality . . . . pluralidad
polarity . . . . polaridad
popularity . . . . popularidad
possibility . . . . **posibilidad**
    "There's a lot of possibility." . . . **"Hay mucha posibilidad".**
posterity . . . . posteridad
priority . . . . prioridad
probability . . . . probabilidad
productivity . . . . productividad
profundity . . . . profundidad
promiscuity . . . . promiscuidad
property . . . . propiedad
prosperity . . . . prosperidad
proximity . . . . proximidad
puberty . . . . pubertad
publicity . . . . publicidad *(also used for "advertising")*
punctuality . . . . puntualidad

quality . . . . **calidad**
quantity . . . . **cantidad**

rationality . . . . racionalidad
reality . . . . realidad
regularity . . . . regularidad
relativity . . . . relatividad
respectability . . . . respetabilidad

responsibility. . . . . **responsabilidad**
  "Whose responsibility is it?" . . . **"¿De quién es la**
                                       responsabilidad?"

sanity. . . . . sanidad *(meaning "general health")*
security. . . . . seguridad
selectivity . . . . selectividad
senility . . . . senilidad
sensibility . . . . sensibilidad
sensitivity . . . . sensibilidad
sensuality . . . . sensualidad
serenity . . . . serenidad
severity. . . . . severidad
sexuality. . . . . sexualidad
similarity. . . . . similaridad
simplicity . . . . simplicidad
sincerity . . . . sinceridad
singularity. . . . . singularidad
sobriety . . . . sobriedad
society . . . . sociedad
solidarity . . . . solidaridad
solubility. . . . . solubilidad
speciality . . . . **especialidad**
spirituality. . . . . espiritualidad
spontaneity. . . . . espontaneidad
stability . . . . estabilidad
sterility . . . . esterilidad
subjectivity . . . . subjetividad
superficiality . . . . superficialidad
superiority . . . . superioridad

temerity . . . . temeridad
temporality . . . . temporalidad
tenacity . . . . tenacidad
tonality. . . . . tonalidad
totality . . . . totalidad

tranquility . . . . tranquilidad
trinity . . . . trinidad
triviality . . . . trivialidad

ubiquity . . . . ubicuidad
uniformity . . . . uniformidad
unity . . . . unidad
universality . . . . universalidad
university . . . . **universidad**
   "It's a good university." . . . . . **"Es una buena universidad".**
utility . . . . utilidad *(meaning "usefulness")*

vanity. . . . . vanidad
variability . . . . variabilidad
variety . . . . variedad
velocity. . . . . velocidad
verity . . . . verdad *(meaning "truth")*
versatility . . . . versatilidad
viability . . . . viabilidad
vicinity . . . . vecindad
virginity . . . . virginidad
virility. . . . . virilidad
virtuality . . . . virtualidad
viscosity . . . . viscosidad
visibility . . . . **visibilidad**
vitality . . . . vitalidad
vivacity. . . . . vivacidad
volatility . . . . volatilidad
voracity . . . . voracidad
vulgarity. . . . . vulgaridad
vulnerability . . . . vulnerabilidad

24A.

Una las palabras que están relacionadas o que son sinónimos.

1. calidad	excelencia
2. creatividad	luz
3. personalidad	abundancia
4. universidad	arte
5. cantidad	carácter
6. electricidad	infinito
7. eternidad	profesora

24B.

Escuche y lea el cuento. Responda las siguientes preguntas, usando oraciones completas.

La última ciudad para Juan y Angélica es La Coruña. Angélica está muy entusiasmada; dice que La Coruña es una <u>ciudad</u> con mucha <u>creatividad</u> y <u>actividad</u>. Juan dice que le gusta mucho la <u>personalidad</u> de este lugar. No tienen mucha <u>dificultad</u> en andar por las calles y puentes (bridges) **de la <u>ciudad</u>. La Coruña es una bella <u>comunidad</u> y ellos permanecen allí** (they stay there) **por cuatro días. Un día Angélica cree ver** (she thinks she sees) **una <u>celebridad</u>: Antonio Banderas. Pero Juan dice que es una <u>imposibilidad</u>, porque Banderas está filmando una película en Suiza. Antes de partir a casa, Juan dice, "Angélica, tengo una pregunta, podemos vivir aquí en La Coruña algún día?" Angélica responde, "Sí, sí, hay muchas <u>posibilidades</u> para nosotros aquí. Veremos...".**

1. ¿Qué dice Angélica de La Coruña?

2. ¿Qué le gusta a Juan de esta ciudad?

3. ¿Tienen dificultad en andar por La Coruña?

4. ¿Angélica ve a una celebridad?

5. ¿Quiere Angélica vivir en La Coruña algún día? ¿Qué dice?

ANSWER KEY

1A.

1. animal: gato
2. personal: privado
3. artificial: sintético
4. crucial: importante
5. ideal: perfecto
6. legal: contrato
7. final: terminar

1B.

1. Juan y Angélica son de Bilbao.
2. Juan quiere hacer un viaje internacional.
3. Angélica quiere hacer un viaje nacional.
4. Juan dice que la idea de Angélica no es original.
5. Según Juan, el tío de Angélica es demasiado formal y tradicional.

2A.

1. fragancia: perfume
2. distancia: lejos
3. perseverancia: constancia
4. tolerancia: paciencia
5. arrogancia: soberbia
6. ambulancia: hospital
7. importancia: significado

2B.

1. Juan habla de la importancia de no gastar mucho.
2. Juan no tiene mucha tolerancia hacia el mundo "chic".
3. La perseverancia será necesaria.
4. Sí, Angélica entiende la importancia de no gastar mucho dinero.
5. Juan responde, "Veremos".

3A.

1. ignorante: desconocedor
2. elegante: fino
3. importante: esencial
4. elefante: animal
5. arrogante: pretencioso
6. flagrante: evidente
7. restaurante: cafetería

3B.

1. Van a Barcelona
2. Angélica piensa que la gente de Barcelona es arrogante.
3. Juan dice que el modo de vestir de la gente de Barcelona es muy elegante.
4. Juan dice que la historia de Barcelona es muy importante.
5. El restaurante de Andrés se llama El Elefante Rojo.

4A.

1. cardiovascular: corazón
2. regular: constante
3. singular: único
4. circular: redondo
5. similar: parecido
6. dólar: moneda
7. nuclear: atómico

4B.

1. Van a una lección de italiano mientras están en Barcelona.
2. Andrés estudia italiano porque el italiano es muy popular en Ibiza, y quiere trabajar en Ibiza.
3. El profesor habla de muchos verbos irregulares.
4. Los tres amigos hablan de la diferencia entre el singular y el plural en el italiano.
5. No, Angélica piensa que el italiano es muy irregular (difícil).

5A.

1. aniversario: cumpleaños
2. salario: dinero
3. necesario: vital
4. vocabulario: palabras
5. itinerario: ruta
6. ordinario: común
7. contrario: opuesto

5B.

1. El itinerario de Juan y Angélica es muy intenso en Barcelona.
2. Angélica quiere comprar un diario.
3. Angélica escribe mucho/todo/cada detalle en su diario.
4. Juan dice que el ritmo es extraordinario.
5. Según Juan, no es necesario escribir cada detalle en el diario.

6A.

1. flexible: elástico
2. terrible: horrible
3. probable: posible
4. estable: seguro
5. inflexible: rígido
6. miserable: infeliz
7. adorable: bonito

6B.

1. Después de Barcelona van a Valencia.
2. Angélica piensa que Juan es muy irresponsable.
3. Juan dice que Angélica es inflexible.
4. Angélica piensa que es (bastante) improbable que regresen a Valencia algún día.
5. Al final, Angélica pregunta si será posible comprar los boletos en Valencia.

7A.

1. correcto: bien
2. perfecto: ideal
3. incorrecto: mal
4. dialecto: idioma
5. acto: teatro
6. aspecto: parte
7. insecto: mosca

7B.

1. Tomaron el tren directo de Barcelona a Valencia.
2. Angélica piensa que no es el lugar correcto porque no comprende nada.
3. Angélica no comprende el español en Valencia porque hay un acento fuerte.
4. El contacto de Juan en Valencia se llama Alfonso.
5. La salsa de Alfonso estuvo perfecta.

8A.

1. paciencia: esperar
2. conferencia: reunión
3. residencia: casa
4. diferencia: distinción
5. violencia: guerra
6. evidencia: prueba
7. independencia: liberación

8B.

1. Alfonso dice que él y su novia van al baile mañana por la noche.
2. Según Angélica la persistencia y diligencia ayudan.
3. Juan piensa que el baile será una buena experiencia.
4. A Juan el baile le causa indiferencia.
5. Juan pide disculpas por su impaciencia.

INSTANT Spanish Vocabulary Builder

9A.

1. permanente: fijo
2. reciente: nuevo
3. diferente: distinto
4. presidente: jefe
5. evidente: obvio
6. residente: habitante
7. presente: actual

9B.

1. Angélica recibe un mensaje urgente.
2. Diego es el presidente de una compañia médica.
3. Angélica dice que su primo es diferente (inteligente/un médico competente).
4. Según Angélica, Diego es muy inteligente.
5. Al final Juan dice, "Está bien, veremos".

10A.

1. biología: vida
2. radiología: rayos X
3. tecnología: computadora
4. trilogía: tres
5. estrategia: plan
6. cronología: historia
7. geología: tierra

10B.

1. Diego tiene mucha energía.
2. Los muchachos no tienen alergia al café.
3. Diego habla de nuevas tecnologías.
4. Juan nunca ha estudiado radiología.
5. Angélica no estudia psicología.

11A.

1. pragmático: práctico
2. tráfico: carros
3. auténtico: verdadero
4. específico: detalles
5. electrónico: estéreo
6. clásico: intemporal
7. romántico: amoroso

11B.

1. Hay mucho tráfico.
2. Angélica dice que el tren es mejor porque no es muy romántico pasar las vacaciones dentro de un carro.
3. Van a algunos museos artísticos.
4. Alicante es mágico por la noche.
5. Alicante es una ciudad fantástica.

12A.

1. típico: usual
2. idéntico: igual
3. práctico: pragmático
4. biográfico: personal
5. diabólico: demoníaco
6. clínico: médico
7. crítico: importante

12B.

1. Juan quiere permanacer en Alicante.
2. Angélica quiere viajar de una manera lógica.
3. Sí, Angélica es siempre práctica.
4. Van a la Costa del Sol.
5. Angélica dice, "Tú también quieres ir a la Costa del Sol, ¿verdad?"

13A.

1. rápido: veloz
2. tímido: introvertido
3. estúpido: idiota
4. ácido: limón
5. frígido: helado
6. árido: seco
7. espléndido: maravilloso

13B.

1. Angélica dice que es un plan estúpido.
2. Juan piensa que es un plan (idea) espléndido.
3. Hace calor (muy húmedo) durante el viaje.
4. Angélica le compra un poco de antiácido para Juan cuando él se siente mal.
5. El farmacéutico dice que debe beber mucho líquido y no comer comida ácida.

14A.

1. turismo: vacaciones
2. comunismo: Karl Marx
3. patriotismo: nación
4. atletismo: olímpico
5. terrorismo: bomba
6. optimismo: positivo
7. criticismo: comentario

14B.

1. Sí, hay mucho turismo en la Costa del Sol.
2. El fascismo comenzó durante los años treinta.
3. Angélica lee sobre la influencia del comunismo y del socialismo en España.
4. Ellos hablan sobre el patriotismo español.
5. Al final Juan dice, "¡Tomemos un helado!"

15A.

1. artista: cantante
2. dentista: diente
3. turista: pasaporte
4. pesimista: negativo
5. idealista: positivo
6. finalista: campeón
7. capitalista: dinero

15B.

1. El muchacho es dentista.
2. Sí, los nuevos amigos de Juan y Angélica viajan a menudo.
3. Angélica tiene una lista de preguntas.
4. El dentista es pesimista y es realista.
5. La artista es optimista y es idealista.

16A.

1. creativo: imaginativo
2. consecutivo: siguiente
3. negativo: pesimista
4. positivo: optimista
5. competitivo: ganador
6. productivo: eficiente
7. motivo: causa

16B.

1. Juan había escuchado muchas cosas negativas sobre Andalucía.
2. Juan piensa que (ve) Andalucía es absolutamente fascinante.
3. Angélica tiene una impresión positiva de Andalucía.
4. El pueblo de Jerez es poco activo pero muy acogedor.
5. Pasan dos días consecutivos allí.

17A.

1. instrumento: guitarra
2. apartamento: renta
3. momento: instante
4. documento: papel
5. tratamiento: medicina
6. segmento: parte
7. monumento: héroes

17B.

1. El argumento en camino hacia el norte es si ir a Córdoba o no.
2. El tío de Angélica vive en Córdoba.
3. Su tío es profesor.
4. Juan no quiere ir a Córdoba porque el tío de Angélica siempre tiene algún comentario sobre el compartamiento de ellos (él es muy formal y nunca da un halago).
5. Sí, al final, deciden ir a Córdoba.

18A.

1. motor: coche
2. color: verde
3. favor: gracias
4. terror: horror
5. autor: libro
6. inventor: patente
7. exterior: afuera

18B.

1. Angélica nota el terror en la cara de Juan.
2. Juan dice, "¡Qué error venir aquí!" sobre la decisión de ir a Córdoba.
3. Juan dice, "Dime que no debo ir a esa fiesta".
4. No, el actor no es famoso.
5. No, el senador es muy, muy viejo.

19A.

1. accesorio: aretes
2. territorio: zona
3. dormitorio: cama
4. laboratorio: experimento
5. observatorio: telescopio
6. derogatorio: insulto
7. introductorio: prólogo

19B.

1. Después de Córdoba van a Sevilla.
2. Juan hubiera preferido un hostal.
3. Juan dice que la fiesta fue peor que el purgatorio.
4. No, no es verdad que su presencia no era obligatoria.
5. No, Juan no responde al último comentario contradictorio de Angélica.

20A.

1. curioso: inquisitivo
2. famoso: celebridad
3. delicioso: sabroso
4. misterioso: suspenso
5. furioso: enojado
6. precioso: diamante
7. espacioso: amplio

20B.

1. Quieren pasar un fin de semana ambicioso en Sevilla.
2. Sevilla es famosa por los churros deliciosos.
3. El amigo de Juan le dijo que hay un aire misterioso allí.
4. En la Universidad de Sevilla hay un programa famoso de lenguas extranjeras.
5. Su hotel es muy espacioso.

21A.

1. confusión: caos
2. misión: objetivo
3. televisión: antena
4. explosión: bomba
5. pasión: amor
6. precisión: exactitud
7. visión: ojo

21B.

1. La misión de Angélica es encontrar un plato de cerámica.
2. Quiere el plato para su colección.
3. Angélica dice que su decisión es final.
4. Juan tiene la impresión de que Angélica no está bromeando.
5. Había un poco de confusión con todas las callejuelas y callejones.

22A.

1. crisis: dificultad
2. tuberculosis: enfermedad
3. énfasis: acento
4. parálisis: inmovilidad
5. hipnosis: soñar
6. metamorfosis: cambio
7. análisis: estudio

22B.

1. No ponen mucho énfasis en el giro turístico porque ya conocen Madrid bastante bien.
2. Carlos escribe la tesis sobre la crisis financiera del tercer mundo.
3. Sí, Carlos habla largo y tendido sobre su análisis.
4. No, Carlos no tiene una buena hipótesis para su tesis.
5. Carlos pregunta a Juan, "¿Puedes ayudarme?"

23A.

1. información: noticias
2. dirección: a la derecha
3. estación: tren
4. nación: país
5. emoción: sentimiento
6. solución: resultado
7. celebración: fiesta

23B.

1. Ven el anuncio para la celebración en la estación de Salamanca.
2. Esta fiesta será grande.
3. La celebración es importante para Juan porque es la situación perfecta
   para conocer Salamanca y su cocina.
4. La reacción de Angélica es más sobria.
5. Al final de la fiesta Juan está mas tranquilo.

24A.

1. calidad: excelencia
2. creatividad: arte
3. personalidad: carácter
4. universidad: profesora
5. cantidad: abundancia
6. electricidad: luz
7. eternidad: infinito

24B.

1. Angélica dice que La Coruña es una ciudad con mucha creatividad y
   actividad.
2. A Juan le gusta la personalidad de esta ciudad.
3. No, no tienen dificultad en andar por La Coruña.
4. Angélica cree ver a una celebridad.
5. Angélica dice, "Sí, hay muchas posibilidades para nosostros aquí… veremos".

APPENDIX

CD TRACK LISTING

	English suffix	Spanish suffix
Track 1 (3:36)	–al	–al
Track 2 (2:14)	–ance	–ancia
Track 3 (2:41)	–ant	–ante
Track 4 (1:58)	–ar	–ar
Track 5 (2:36)	–ary	–ario
Track 6 (3:58)	–ble	–ble
Track 7 (2:13)	–ct	–cto
Track 8 (3:16)	–ence	–encia
Track 9 (3:01)	–ent	–ente
Track 10 (2:45)	–gy	–gía
Track 11 (4:21)	–ic	–ico
Track 12 (2:23)	–ical	–ico
Track 13 (1:46)	–id	–ido
Track 14 (3:04)	–ism	–ismo
Track 15 (3:16)	–ist	–ista
Track 16 (3:19)	–ive	–ivo
Track 17 (2:20)	–ment	–mento
Track 18 (3:18)	–or	–or
Track 19 (1:50)	–ory	–orio
Track 20 (2:48)	–ous	–oso
Track 21 (3:03)	–sion	–sión
Track 22 (2:13)	–sis	–sis
Track 23 (5:05)	–tion	–ción
Track 24 (3:57)	–ty	–dad
Track 25 (1:18)	Pronunciation Guide	

ABOUT THE AUTHOR

Tom Means is an instructor in the Italian Department at Rutgers University, New Jersey. He owns and operates a private language school in New York City, the Means Language Center, where he conducts Spanish, French, and Italian classes for international companies and private clients.

ALSO AVAILABLE FROM HIPPOCRENE BOOKS...

INSTANT FRENCH VOCABULARY BUILDER
CD • 4,000 ENTRIES • 216 PAGES • 6 X 9 • 0-7818-0982-7 • $14.95PB • (485)

INSTANT ITALIAN VOCABULARY BUILDER
CD • 4,000 ENTRIES • 224 PAGES • 6 X 9 • 0-7818-0980-0 • $14.95PB • (476)

Instantly add thousands of words to your French or Italian using word-ending patterns! Many words in French and Italian are nearly the same as their English counterparts due to their common Latin origin. The only difference is the word ending. For example, you can translate most English words ending in –ous (such as "mysterious") into French by changing the ending to –eux ("mystéri–*uex*") and into Italian by changing the ending to –oso ("misteri–*oso*"). Because each of these patterns applies to hundreds of words, by learning them you can increase your vocabulary instantly.

In each book of this unique series, Tom Means describes the most common 23 or 24 word-ending patterns for the target language and provides over 4,000 words that follow them. On the accompanying CD, a native speaker demonstrates correct pronunciation of each chapter's most commonly used words and phrases.

Only language acquisition books that use word-ending patterns

■

Over 4,000 vocabulary words in each book

■

Exercises at end of each chapter

■

Perfect as classroom supplements or for self-study

■

Companion CDs teach pronunciation

SPANISH INTEREST TITLES FROM HIPPOCRENE BOOKS...

Language Guides

SPANISH-ENGLISH/ENGLISH-SPANISH PRACTICAL DICTIONARY
35,000 ENTRIES • 338 PAGES • 5½ x 8½ • 0-7818-0179-6 • $9.95PB • (211)

SPANISH-ENGLISH/ENGLISH-SPANISH DICTIONARY & PHRASEBOOK (LATIN AMERICAN)
2,000 ENTRIES • 250 PAGES • 3¾ x 7½ • 0-7818-0773-5 • $11.95PB • (261)

EMERGENCY SPANISH PHRASEBOOK
80 PAGES • 7½ x 4⅛ • 0-7818-0977-0 • $5.95PB • (460)

HIPPOCRENE CHILDREN'S ILLUSTRATED SPANISH DICTIONARY
English-Spanish/Spanish-English
- for ages 5 and up
- 500 entries with color pictures
- commonsense pronunciation for each Spanish word
- Spanish-English index

500 ENTRIES • 94 PAGES • 8 x 11 • 0-7818-0889-8 • $11.95PB • (181)

BEGINNER'S SPANISH
313 PAGES • 5½ x 8½ • 0-7818-0840-5 • $14.95PB • (225)

MASTERING ADVANCED SPANISH
326 PAGES • 5½ x 8½ • 0-7818-0081-1 • $14.95PB • (413)
2 CASSETTES: CA. 2 HOURS • 0-7818-0089-7 • $12.95 • (426)

SPANISH GRAMMAR
224 PAGES • 5½ x 8½ • 0-87052-893-9 • $12.95PB • (273)

SPANISH VERBS: SER AND ESTAR
220 PAGES • 5½ x 8½ • 0-7818-0024-2 • $8.95PB • (292)

DICTIONARY OF LATIN AMERICAN SPANISH PHRASES AND EXPRESSIONS
1,900 ENTRIES • 178 PAGES • 5½ x 8½ • 0-7818-0865-0 • $14.95 • (286)

SPANISH PROVERBS, IDIOMS AND SLANG
350 PAGES • 6 x 9 • 0-7818-0675-5 • $14.95PB • (760)

History and Culture

SPAIN: AN ILLUSTRATED HISTORY
Spain has had a remarkable history. It was a thriving center of Islamic civilization for many centuries until its conquest by Christian kings. Before long, this country had expanded to become one of the world's greatest empires, leaving traces of its culture, language, and religion throughout the world. This narrative provides a survey of Spanish history that is perfect for the student, traveler, or generally curious reader.
176 PAGES • 5 x 7 • 50 B/W PHOTOS./ILLUS/MAPS • 0-7818-0874-X • $12.95PB • (339)

MEXICO: AN ILLUSTRATED HISTORY
This historical guide traces Mexico's growth from the days of the Olmecs to the present. With the aid of over 50 illustrations, photos, and maps, the reader will discover how events of Mexico's past have left an indelible mark on the politics, economy, culture, and spirit of this country and its people. The author explores issues of social class, power, dependency, conquest, and the fortitude of this remarkable country.
150 PAGES • 5 x 7 • 50 B/W PHOTOS./ILLUS/MAPS • 0-7818-0690-9 • $11.95HC • (585)

Literature

TREASURY OF SPANISH LOVE POEMS, QUOTATIONS & PROVERBS
In Spanish and English
This classic collection features great Spanish poems and characteristic sayings on the subject of romance. It spans 1500 years of Spanish literature and folklore. Many authors are featured, including Miguel de Cervantes. All works appear in Spanish with facing English translations.
128 PAGES • 5 x 7 • 0-7818-0358-6 • $11.95 • (589)
2 CASSETTES: CA. 2 HOURS • $12.95 • (584) • 0-7818-0365-9

TREASURY OF SPANISH LOVE SHORT STORIES
In Spanish and English
A perfect gift for a loved one, this volume features side-by-side Spanish and English.
157 PAGES • 5 x 7 • 0-7818-0298-9 • $11.95 • (604)

Treasury of Mexican Love Poems, Quotations & Proverbs
In Spanish and English
This beautiful anthology captures the many varieties of love in Mexican literature. Its selections include passionate works by Sor Juana de la Cruz, postmodern verse by Ramón López Velarde, and the contemporary poetry of Rosario Castellanos. All works appear in Spanish with facing English translations.
150 PAGES • 5 X 7 • 0-7818-0985-1 • $11.95HC • (495)

Folk Tales from Chile
These classic stories will delight young and old readers. This unique collection of fifteen folk tales represents a fusion of two cultures—the Old World culture of the Spanish soldiers and priests, and the native culture of Chile's original inhabitants.
121 PAGES • 5 X 8 • 15 ILLUSTRATIONS • 0-7818-0712-3 • $12.50HC • (785)

Dictionary of 1,000 Spanish Proverbs
Organized alphabetically by key words, this bilingual reference book is a guide to and information source for a key element of Spanish.
131 PAGES • 5½ X 8½ • 0-7818-0412-4 • $11.95PB • (254)

Cuisine

A Spanish Family Cookbook, Revised Edition
244 PAGES • 5½ X 8½ • 0-7818-0546-5 • $11.95PB • (642)

Tastes of the Pyrenees, Classic and Modern
This cookbook focuses on the polyglot of cuisines of the Pyrenees region, whose mountains stretch almost 300 miles from the balmy beaches of the Mediterranean to the turbulent Atlantic coast. The recipes in this book include ones from Catalonia in both Spain and France, Roussillon, Languedoc, the Midi Pyrenees, the Basque country (*Euskal Herria*) in both France and Spain, Asturias, Navarra, and Aragón. It also includes chapters on the natural and human history that provide a background for today's cuisines of the Pyrenees. Each of the 86 recipes opens with a short narrative introduction that highlights the differences and similarities in the various cooking styles of this exciting culinary region.
296 PAGES • 6 X 9 • TWO-COLOR • 0-7818-0949-5 • $24.95HC • (405)

OLD HAVANA COOKBOOK
Cuban Recipes in Spanish and English
Cuban cuisine, though derived from its mother country, Spain, has been modified and refined by locally available foods like pork, rice, corn, beans and sugar, and the requirements of a tropical climate. This cookbook includes over 50 recipes, each in Spanish with side-by-side English translation—all of them adapted for the North American kitchen. Among the recipes included are: Ajiaco (famous Cuban Stew), Boiled Pargo with Avocado Sauce, Lobster Havanaise, Tamal en Cazuela (Soft Tamal), Quimbombó (okra), Picadillo, Roast Suckling Pig, and Boniatillo (Sweet Potato Dulce), along with a whole chapter on famous Cuban cocktails and beverages.
123 PAGES • 5 x 7 • LINE DRAWINGS • 0-7818-0767-0 • $11.95HC • (590)

TASTES OF PERU
The food of Peru is dominated by the "sun" cuisine of the Incas, whose love of everything yellow is legendary. The most popular dish, ceviche, is made of fish, shrimp, or scallops marinated in lime juice. In this cookbook, 130 Peruvian recipes are accompanied by a glossary of ingredients and their availability.
200 PAGES • 6 x 9 • TWO-COLOR • $24.95HC • 0-7818-0965-7 • (532)

THE ART OF BRAZILIAN COOKERY
In the 40 years since its original publication, *The Art of Brazilian Cookery* has been a trusted source for home chefs through the decades. This authentic cookbook of Brazilian food, the first of its kind to be published in the U.S., includes over 300 savory and varied recipes and begins with a vivid historical-geographic and culinary picture of Brazil.
240 PAGES • 5½ x 8¼ • 0-7818-0130-3 • $11.95PB • (250)

Prices subject to change without prior notice. To purchase Hippocrene Books contact your local bookstore, call (718) 454-2366, or write to: **HIPPOCRENE BOOKS**, 171 Madison Avenue, New York, NY 10016. Please enclose check or money order, adding $5.00 shipping (UPS) for the first book, and $.50 for each additional book.